The Politics of Race

Hillel Ticktin

The Politics of Race:
Discrimination in South Africa

Hillel Ticktin

PLUTO PRESS
London • Concord, Mass

First published in 1991 by Pluto Press
345 Archway Road, London, N6 5AA
and 141 Old Bedford Road,
Concord, MA 01742, USA

British Library Cataloguing-in-Publication Data
Ticktin, Hillel *1937–*
> The politics of race: discrimination in South Africa.
> 1. South Africa. Black persons. Racial discrimination by
> society. Political aspects.
> I. Title
> 323.11968I

> ISBN 0–7453–0494–X

Library of Congress Cataloging-in-Publication Data
Ticktin, H. (Hillel)
> The politics of race: discrimination in South Africa / Hillel
> Ticktin.
>> p. cm.
> Includes bibliographical references and index.
> ISBN 0–7453–0494–X.
> 1. Race discrimination – South Africa. 2. Capitalism – South
> Africa. 3. Socialism – South Africa. 4. Social conflict – South
> Africa. 5. South Africa – Race relations. I. Title.
> DT1756.T53   1991
> 305.8'00968–dc20   90–49040
>   CIP

Typeset by Stanford Desktop Publishing Services, Milton Keynes
Printed and bound in the UK by Billing and Sons Ltd, Worcester

Contents

List of Tables

Introduction

This little book has its own long genesis. Many of the basic ideas were part of a thesis written in the Department of Political Economy of the Faculty of Economics at Moscow University during the years 1961–5. At that time the USSR was very much within a Stalinist straitjacket, even though Khrushchev was in power until 1964. My supervisor, M.S. Dragilev, a Professor of 'Imperialism', was almost literally afraid of his own shadow. He had been dismissed from his job during the time of the purges and reduced to a barber. No doubt for that reason he would not sign any of the numerous documents that I needed to have signed, if he could possibly avoid it. All the more did he object to my thesis which he saw as being very controversial in that it contradicted the official line of the Communist Party of that time.

I argued that racial discrimination had to be seen as a form of superexploitation of a section of the working class. Superexploitation, in turn, had to be seen as part of capitalism itself. The division of the working class into a privileged and less privileged section facilitated the continuity of capitalism by employing the antagonism of the privileged whites towards the less privileged blacks. I had pointed to the particular role of the Irish workers in the nineteenth century, which had so exercised Marx and Engels, to illustrate my argument. Given the nature of the Soviet Union of the time, where all works in political economy had to be buttressed with quotations from Marx, Engels and Lenin, this rather surprised the members of the faculty. They had no reply. We agreed to leave the matter of my thesis as it stood.

In fact, of course, the ideas themselves were not particularly original, being part of the common wisdom of much of the left movement of South Africa, from which I had originated. I was very much indebted both to Professor Jack Simons and Dr. Baruch Hirson, who at that time were teaching at Cape Town and Witwatersrand universities respectively. The originality, such as it was, lay in the attempt to provide a general theory of racial discrimination based on Marxist political economy.

Thereafter I came to Britain and switched my focus much more on to the political economy of the USSR and more general problems of Marxist political economy. While giving lectures and writing odd articles on South Africa over the next twenty years, I did not set about systematically rewriting the ideas of the thesis until 1986, when I was

1

asked by the editors of an American journal to write an article on South Africa for their readers. I realized that a simple description of events in South Africa would not provide much understanding of what was happening there and therefore tried to provide a theoretical background to the revolutionary situation of 1984–6. It turned out, however, that such a theory could not really be encompassed in the space of a short article, so I enlarged the piece until it turned into a short book.

The crucial question, around which all debates in South Africa have hinged, is the interrelation between capitalism, socialism and racial discrimination. Already in the 1920s, the Communist Party had divided on that issue. One of its founders, S.P. Bunting, was arguing against the Bukharinist official line of the Communist International (Comintern) of 1928 for a Black Republic. He asserted that the struggle in South Africa was a classical one in which the black working class would have to emancipate itself by taking power and beginning the transition to socialism.[1] The Bukharinist line became the official line of the South African Communist Party over the years, leading ultimately to its lineal descendant, the theory of internal colonialism. On the other hand, the Trotskyist movement, which came to be as strong if not stronger than the Communist Party at one point, also split on similar lines. The Unity Movement, the main Trotskyist group,[2] took its cue from Trotsky, who had answered a letter from one of its members, by stressing the importance of racial discrimination, and it emphasized the need for a transitional anti-racialist programme.

By the early 1960s black nationalism appeared victorious. Only with the emergence of black unions and with the growth of strikes by black workers did activists' attitudes to change in South Africa begin to alter. This book is an attempt to discuss, theoretically, the nature of racial discrimination, as a feature of modern capitalism, in the context of South Africa. Although there is a reference to history, that is only in the context of the discovery of the origins of the crucial categories of racial discrimination in South Africa.

History can be perceived as a movement of and change in institutions, social groups, organizations, policies and ideas or as an interaction of consciousness with underlying categories, which have to be discovered by painstaking theoretical and empirical work. The categories themselves, however, cannot be detected by simple empirical work. Their correctness can only be discovered by the extent to which they explain events over time. It may be that certain of the necessary categories, sub-categories and laws can never be empirically substantiated. That does not mean that empirical work is of no value but it does mean that to understand change we must look for the underlying causes of movement. That is what this book is about.

The Russian Revolution and its Stalinization has played a crucial role in the events of the twentieth century. I take the view that South Africa cannot be understood outside that context.

The first four chapters are to be understood as laying a theoretical groundwork. The first chapter defines essential categories and terms. The second chapter goes into a theory of racial discrimination by briefly discussing other views and explaining the particular theory adopted in the book. That view is then outlined in more detail in the next two chapters. To summarize and simplify the argument, racial discrimination is seen as a modern phenomenon, only possible under conditions of industrialization. Racial discrimination divides the workers, so preventing the formation of a class under conditions when industrialization tends towards the formation of a relatively homogeneous mass of workers. It performs this act by paying the discriminated workers below the value of their labour power, while paying white workers more than the value of their labour power. The difference between South Africa and other countries where such discrimination exists lies in the fact that the majority is discriminated against, so permitting a relatively few white workers to have much higher pay. The extent of such a transfer is critical in discussing the role and position of the white workers.

Racial discrimination became official government policy, as opposed to a spontaneous practice, in the period after 1922. It is argued here that it can only be understood as a response to the white workers' strike of 1922. While it is perfectly possible to show a continuous history of racial discrimination in the South African economy and society, it is argued that a watershed was reached by the early 1920s. History is a record of discontinuities within continuities. It is the task of theory to discover those discontinuities. The continuities are usually easily detected even if not easily traced out. It is argued that in the context of a world situation where capitalism was under threat, Britain and the British mineowners preferred to concede to white workers and the Afrikaner farmers rather than take on a united working class.

In the following chapter, on Capital in South Africa, the consequences are traced out. Racial discrimination, of which apartheid is a particular form, is inefficient and so costly to capital, to the point where it is doubtful if it has any economic gain at all from cheap black labour. The forms of capital, themselves, take on a racial hue. While capital itself is colour blind and gender blind, nonetheless, in actually existing capitalism, capital itself operates with distorted categories. The nature of the South African economy, its branches and degree of mechanization are all closely related to racial discrimination. On the one hand, Marxists argue that the state is the organ of repression of the ruling class, while on the other hand the South African state appears to be acting against the interests of the capitalist class. The state, however, is serving the purpose of repressing any revolt against capitalism, while at the same time it is subordinating the direction of capital in order to achieve that purpose. The peculiar form of the South African state can only be understood in a global context, where not only has capitalism been historically overthrown in a part of the world but that rejection of capitalism took on a Stalinist form.

The following chapter, on Labour, discusses the nature of the interrelation of black and white labour. For this purpose it abstracts from the different divisions within the black working class. It asks the question of the nature of labour in South Africa. It shows the working-class (as opposed to peasant) nature of South Africa and the differential divisions among the white workers. The chapter discusses in some detail the concept of abstract labour and its fracturing to understand the particular nature of South African capital.

The following chapter discusses the nature of contemporary solutions to the crisis in South Africa. It shows that the almost certain result will be one in which formal racial discrimination is abolished in favour of a black middle class but the black working class will remain in the same fundamental structural position as before.

The next chapter puts South Africa in a world context, and discusses its relationship with imperialism and the world economy. It takes the view that the South African capitalist class can only be defined in relation to the world economy. It rejects the doctrine that the whites preside over an internal colony.

The chapter on the national question and consciousness argues that there is effectively one nation in South Africa, with different national groups, but that it is in the nature of capitalism to produce a distorted consciousness. Commodity fetishism, it is argued, is crucial in understanding the formation of nationalism and racialist ideology.

The final chapter argues that the settlement in South Africa has been worked out by the Great Powers. Everything will be done to avoid socialism. While the immediate result will indeed be a form of agreement with blacks holding a great measure of political power, the economy will necessarily remain both capitalist and largely white controlled. In this respect events in the USSR and Eastern Europe must play a role. The socialist alternative is set out.

1
The Debates in South Africa

The general laws of political economy apply as much to South Africa as to other parts of the capitalist world, but they are refracted through the category of racial discrimination. In this regard, there are three problems that have to be addressed. The first is the particular role of racial discrimination in the history, politics and production relations of South Africa. The second involves the respective roles of the state and capitalist class in the maintenance of racial discrimination. This then leads to a third – political – question. Will the South African revolution be a one-stage or two-stage revolution and will it be community or worker based? In other words, should the struggle be based on working-class forms or on nationalist cum guerilla forms?

This book is intended to be an introduction to these debates. The thesis put forward here is that the peculiar social relations of South Africa are to be understood as a twentieth century solution to the capital/worker relation. Just as the 'white Australia' policy was a labour policy in opposition to the attempt by capital to undercut wages, so too the white supremacy policy in South Africa derives from white labour politics. Historically, the capitalist class accepted the demands of white labour because it was internationally too weak to do otherwise.

The crucial theoretical issue, therefore, is that of the nature of the division of the workforce and the relation of the capitalist class to the different sections of its workforce.[3] On the one hand, the capitalist class appears to have cheap black labour by employing the whites as a praetorian guard. On the other, the capitalist class has to suffer all the expenses and restrictions on accumulation consequent on racial discrimination. To understand this ambiguous relationship it is essential to introduce the category of abstract labour.

The term abstract labour is itself not an easy category but it is a fundamental one. Specifically it refers to the social reduction of labour to a common form. This does not imply that there is an actual physically determined amount of labour time common to all workers. It refers rather to a level of labour time, intensity of labour etc., which is common in the economy. Thus in the United Kingdom the intensity of labour is very different from that of the United States, as is the

5

number of hours worked, the numbers of workers per machine and so on. The question is not that everyone works at the same level but that they tend towards that level. Its determination is a result of the process of accumulation expressed particularly in the mechanization of the economy and of the class struggle. The word form, here, is crucial. The form of abstract labour, hitherto, has tended to be a national form, rather than an international form. In turn, this is reflected in the national fluidity and mobility of labour.[4] The problem in South Africa is that abstract labour has necessarily to be fractured to maintain the system. There are two important consequences. Firstly, the capitalist class faces a conflict between its (individual and collective) economic interests and its collective political interests. Secondly, the fracturing of abstract labour has inevitably led to a community-based form of struggle as opposed to class action. However, the conflict between the formation of abstract labour and its fracturing has only delayed and hindered but cannot prevent the formation of a black working class.

Thus, the fundamental reason that has prevented direct working-class forms of struggle in South Africa is the fracturing of abstract labour. In practice, this material fracturing has provided the opportunity for the African National Congress/Communist Party, and other organizations to turn the community struggle into a nationalist form. The combination of these two forces – the one material and the other political and ideological – has prevented direct working-class forms of struggle. The present nationalist form of the movement (although some workers did advance socialist demands), the nature of the uprising from 1984 onwards, and the consequent defeat are all attributable to the Stalinist leadership and ideology accepted by the masses. In other words, the absence of an anti-capitalist mass movement is to be explained in part by the line of the Communist Party and the influence of the USSR. Indeed, the failure of the campaigns from 1984 onwards may also be traced to the communitarian as opposed to class form of the struggle.

The defeat of 1984–6 and the current strategy of the ruling class necessitates a debate about the nature, development and decay of racial discrimination and its specific adaptation of the laws of capitalism. The simplistic and wrong view that apartheid is a system utilized by the capitalist class to raise its profits has been widely propagated.[5] It has never explained why the capitalist class has always been opposed to the white worker and his extreme racialism, why it financed political opposition to the Nationalist Party and fought to replace white with black workers in the whole period down to 1922. The current Communist Party view that the system exists in order to raise the profits of world imperialism from an 'internal colony' has become common parlance among the left. Unfortunately, the early tradition of theoretical discussion in South Africa on the left, even within the South African Communist Party, has been replaced with descriptive analysis, the gathering of empirical data and ruinous Althusserian diversions.[6]

This unfortunate decline of Marxist analysis has left the way open to liberal interpretations.[7] In a work, very much a social democratic defence of progressive capitalism, one author has correctly described the trials and tribulations of the left in coping with the problem of the role of the capitalist class.[8] Merle Lipton, like many economists, provides historical detail of the costs of apartheid to capital.

This book then attempts to make a non-Stalinist Marxist analysis of South African political economy. For this purpose, it begins with a discussion of theories of racial discrimination and outlines the theory informing this book. It then provides a brief history relevant to the theory. Chapters on the nature of Capital in South Africa and then on the nature of Labour follow. These chapters are succeeded by one which deals with the programmes of political parties as well as the forms of change proposed and introduced by the state. The position of South Africa in the world economy follows and the last two chapters discuss the question of consciousness and alternative strategies for change.

2
The Political Economy of Racial Discrimination

The Categories of Political Economy

Four categories have to be elaborated and understood in order to develop a cogent political economy of South Africa: abstract labour, the decline of capitalism, class, and control over the surplus product.

Abstract labour has already been referred to and will be further discussed below. Therefore the category of decline will be discussed first. An expanding capitalism opposes all limitations on accumulation, especially those that fracture abstract labour. A capitalism, however, which can foresee its own overthrow needs to limit and contain accumulation in such a way that it maximizes its own life even at the expense of the law of value or of profits. Modern capitalism uses nationalization, bureaucratic forms of economic control, and divisions of the working class, all of which run counter to the drive for private accumulation. Racial discrimination has to be seen in this context. The final form of a declining capitalism is that of finance capital which is not interested in the source of its profits, whether the productive sector grows or declines, but only in profits themselves. A parasitic form of capital, it can accept forms of control over capital and labour which limit accumulation, as long as returns are provided. The fact that the productive sector may be destroyed over time is of less interest to finance capital.

The third important category is that of class. Clearly if class is defined as all those who have the same position in relation to the means of production then it is hard to understand the nature of the South African working class, since most whites, white collar and blue collar, are part of it, in addition to the blacks. On the other hand, if class is understood as a collectivity then the whites are excluded from the working class by their different material position. If the collectivity is defined in relation to control over labour power or conversely the sale of labour power then the whites are further excluded, since the white workers are in fact distinguished by their police role in relation to the black workers. Whites in manual and non-manual positions are often in charge of black workers, as in the mining industry. If they are not in control of black workers they may be administering the surplus product, through finance and banking, or they may be part of the bureaucratic apparatus in the state sector, which is in control of a proportion of the surplus product.

This leads logically to a discussion of the surplus product. The form of the surplus product under capitalism is, of course, surplus value. The expansion of value takes the form of the extraction of surplus value from labour. While the worker receives the price of his labour power, the rest of the labour time expended becomes surplus labour time appropriated by the capitalist. The struggle between capital and labour is then over control of that surplus product. In the case of South Africa, the expansion of value and so surplus value has been partially diverted by cession to white workers of a limited degree of control over the process of extraction of surplus value from black workers.

These four categories are closely interlinked and the discussion below will attempt to show how their operation can illuminate the political economy of South Africa. The political economy of any country reflects the way in which it has adapted the contradictions of capitalism that are specific to that region. In the case of South Africa the role of racial discrimination is the key to understanding the particular mediations of the laws of motion of capitalism.

Theories of Racial Discrimination

Racial discrimination in South Africa is not some ideological prejudice imported from Europe, still less is it a throwback from feudalism or early capitalism as many prefer to see it. It is, rather, a rational alternative to the welfare state in maintaining the continued existence of capitalism, under conditions where it would otherwise be overthrown. Racial discrimination, in this understanding, is a modern response utilizing forms and doctrines of an earlier period. Just as the anti-semitism of the past century can only be understood in the context of a dying capitalism, so racial discrimination in South Africa can only be appreciated in a context where a declining capitalist class accepted a policy to which they were opposed, rather than lose all.

A number of different theories of racial discrimination have been advanced. It is useful to provide an outline of the main doctrines in order to provide the background for the theory being put forward here.

The first and common viewpoint is that racial discrimination is a pre-capitalist hangover. It may be perceived as deriving from feudalism, slavery or some other non-capitalist form. The author J. M. Coetzee, for instance, refers to the apartheid he met on the farm as 'centuries old feudalism'.[9] The strict control over labour is easily misperceived as feudal, or deriving from feudalism. Lipton makes the same error.[10] It is a curious view that turns only the most mature forms of capitalism into capitalism, so that early or declining forms are declared non-capitalist. Only those who believe the apologetics of bourgeois economics can believe that markets are normally free of restraint whether over labour or within capital. Where there has been a shortage or other problem of labour, there have been many forms of control introduced, ranging from those under Fascism to the harsh laws under which the early nineteenth-century British and Irish labourers suffered. Some of these laws were transplanted to South Africa, as for instance the Masters and Servants Acts. Even a Marxist, at one time on the left of the Communist Party, makes the same mistake.[11]

A more complex view of the first kind is expressed by Neville Alexander, who has written extensively on the nature of racial discrimination. He, too, however, by enunciating a theory of colour–caste, has injected a pre-capitalist explanation into a capitalist form. His argument is discussed below in the section on the national question, a theme which he makes his own.[12]

The second standpoint lays stress on the imperialist nature of the control over South Africa. The whites are then basically colonial leftovers maintaining imperial exploitation of the majority of the population. The revolution in South Africa is then an anti-imperialist revolution. Such was the Soviet theory, if it can be called a theory at all. South Africa was considered a third world country under the domination of the United Kingdom and the United States. The Africa Institute in Moscow basically subscribed to this view.[13] Although Moscow has supported the South African Communist Party until recently, it tended to look at South Africa in its own way, as part of the imperialist sphere, with a particular form of imperialist policy. Again, this attitude is discussed later in the section on colonialism and imperialism.

The third view has long been expressed by such as Harold Wolpe, a long-serving though critical supporter of the African National Congress (ANC) leadership and its allies. Accepting the view that there is something called internal colonialism, Wolpe has used Althusserianism to good effect in arguing that there were several interacting modes of production in South Africa.[14] The political result is that the programmatic demands of the revolution are expressed in terms of a nationalist first stage followed by a socialist second stage. This theoretical approach combines elements from the first two in seeing racial discrimination as both pre-capitalist and imperialist. It is the present view of the South African Communist Party. The internal colonialism theory is discussed in a section below.

The fourth view was held by the dominant Trotskyist group, the Unity Movement, until its demise. Its theoreticians laid particular stress on three features of South Africa. They saw the country as essentially peasant and consequently regarded the agricultural question as the 'alpha and omega' of the society. They did not consider the mining proletariat a genuine part of the working class. Only the industrial proletariat could be considered truly revolutionary. In addition, they took the view that no change was possible until Stalinism was defeated in the USSR. As a result, they addressed themselves to immediate anti-racist demands. History came to be rewritten in terms of the Herrenvolk and the peasants. As the Unity Movement had considerable influence in South Africa, especially in Cape Town, their ten point programme has had an enduring effect on the minds of a generation of activists. The bottom line of the Unity Movement theory is that the struggle in South Africa is bourgeois democratic because there are too few industrial workers for socialism to be on the order of the day.

The fifth viewpoint is effectively put forward by Frederick A. Johnstone, in his work *Class, Race and Gold*, where he argues that racial discrimination is only to be understood as part of a class analysis. He details the struggles of the white and black workers down to 1922 but asserts that they are to be understood as 'a class struggle over the distribution of the various costs and benefits deriving to different white groups from the operation of the different class colour bars, an historical manifestation of the diverse socio-economic roots and functions of the system of discrimination, of the contradictions built into it.'[15] He explains that his approach is 'quasi-Marxist, quasi-structural' and that it is only one of many possible approaches.

He is specifically criticized by Neville Alexander, who is discussed below in the section on the national question, for not providing an understanding of the term race. As can be seen, Alexander is right in that Johnstone in no way tries to understand the origins of racial discrimination. He only describes the struggle over the distribution of income. While Johnstone is unique in his overall viewpoint, he does express a popular if crass view held on the left that South Africa is simply a capitalist country and the racialist aspect can be simply subsumed under the class struggle, without being explained. His failure has much to with his structuralism. Not surprisingly Alexander is not entirely uncritical.

Another variant of the view that racial discrimination is there to maintain a particular division of surplus value is the view that it serves simply to provide cheap labour. This view, that it is ' a system of economic, social and political relations designed to produce cheap and controlled black labour, and so generate high rates of profit,'[16] is held quite widely in the society. The authors quoted also point to the privileges of the white workers. I argue against this theory below.

Towards a Political Economy of South Africa

The doctrine of the superiority of one genetically different people over those of another ethnic group is a specific invention of capitalism. That there were manifestations of a similar kind of attitude before capitalism is not in dispute. Under capitalism, however, such racialist attitudes acquired a systematic character to the point where they became part of the ideology of the ruling class and so of the society. One of the first writers to have recognized this relationship was Oliver Cromwell Cox in his well-known work on race.[17] In it he showed the capitalist origins of racialism, but did not explain it. He certainly provided comparisons on a Weberian basis but because of the mixture of Marxism and sociology, description of social relations replaces political economy. There is, furthermore, a difference between racialism and racial discrimination. Racialism is an ideology which arose with the conquest of the 'new world' in the fifteenth century. Racial discrimination (as opposed to racial slavery or extermination, which was originally justified with the doctrine of racialism) can only exist when there is the emergence of a homogeneous labour force. Cox, however, fails to make this crucial distinction. Racial discrimination requires that there should be the potential of mobility as opposed to slavery or mutually competing agricultures. It is of the essence of discrimination that it attempts to freeze the very fluidity which is a necessary feature of a developed labour market. Racial discrimination requires the mobility of labour in order to prevent the oppressed section of the workforce entering occupations reserved for those of a different ethnic group. The effect is to create a group of privileged as opposed to superexploited workers.

Hence the rigidities in the system, the common superiority of the whites, do not derive from previous history or from a shared 'whiteness' or common culture but rather from the need of the capitalist class, in order to survive, to find a means of dividing the working class. Naturally they choose some aspect of real existence and then convert it to their own use. Colour is ideal because it is so visible and historically associated in the Northern European ruling class tradition with everything that is unworthy. Nonetheless they could as well have chosen a tribal division between the Xhosa–Zulu speaking tribes and the Sotho–Tswana tribes if there were no Afrikaners to hand. The Swiss, for instance, are a privileged group against the very large proportion of industrial workers from Italy, Spain etc., who are rightless and citizenless. A genuine class history of the Afrikaners is still to be written. What is certain is that it will show that the formation of the Afrikaner nationality grew enormously in the period in which they were incorporated as a junior partner by the ruling group. The nationalism of the Afrikaners, in other words, owes far more to the farseeing English capitalist class than the Afrikaner nationalists are prepared to admit.

The division of the working class is not an empirical and arbitrary action. It is a considered action under conditions of capitalist decline. The cost of conceding to a section of workers is not lightly undertaken. The fundamental essence of the working class lies in its common subjection to the form of abstract labour. Thereby it is rendered both subject to and collectively dependent on capital. When the capitalist class embarks on the fracturing of abstract labour it cannot predict the outcome unless the fracturing is of a limited kind. The super-exploitation of Irish labour in the United Kingdom which exercised Marx and Engels was of a similar nature to the racial discrimination in South Africa, but it was limited to a small proportion of workers. While very important in dividing the class, it could not be said that the category of Irish and non-Irish applied to all accumulation. In South Africa, on the contrary, racial discrimination is total. It affects the lives of all who live in that country and is crucial in understanding all aspects of accumulation. The acceptance of racial discrimination in these circumstances, though unwanted, has taken place under conditions where it was preferable to the alternative of a united working class threatening to overthrow capitalism.

The fracturing of abstract labour entailed in racial discrimination must politicize all workers since the old method of control through commodity fetishism can no longer be maintained, as value has been partially discarded. Commodity fetishism is a term used by Marx to denote the method of control under capitalism. This is composed of two elements: The real and direct control of capital over labour and the ideology of the supremacy of capital. Put crudely, in a capitalist system, profits come before wages. It is not a question of choice, if there are no profits the firm goes bankrupt and the workers get no wages at all. Workers are reduced to the level of an input into production, on a plane with raw materials and machinery. In contrast, a socialist system would put the population's needs first. Commodity fetishism is also an ideology in so far as people regard profits and so capital and the market as an eternal sytem needed by mankind to ensure its survival. The overall effect is that the whole population is dominated by the capitalist system itself. Put differently capitalism has its own mode of control. (The topic is discussed below in some detail in Chapter 9.) The limitation and transformation of commodity fetishism in South Africa has been a greater price for the capitalist class to pay than the inefficiency which has resulted from the colour bar. The politicization has had the compensatory effect, however, of creating a racial and community conflict rather than a straight class conflict. Such a non-class form of struggle is easier to contain and hold down than a conflict in the factories and central urban areas. The politicization is not, therefore, one of a straight class consciousness and consequently has provided the capitalist class with a period of time with which to change tack. In this respect, as indicated, the Communist Party has played a crucial role in assisting the capitalist class in gently easing South Africa into a less racially orientated capitalism, by its refusal to adopt an anti-capitalist programme.

While commodity fetishism is not retained in the old manner, the new form of racial discrimination and its ideology, racialism, are derivations of that commodity fetishism. If the worker is political, he is political in a fetishized form, a racial and community form. He is not able to see his boss as a capitalist instead of as a white oppressor. A veil is therefore drawn over the form of oppression and the nature of exploitation. Whites are rich apparently by right of conquest and not because they may extract surplus value. Unity of workers is necessary because they are black and not because they all sell their labour power. The veil is torn but not wholly and the politicization which ensues is containable for a period of time.

Capital wants a fluid non-divided workforce when it is operating under its own ideal conditions. In its decline, and indeed decay, it has to contend with a working class which is either intent on the overthrow of the system or is demanding a greater share of the surplus value than is optimal for the system. The solutions adopted amount to new forms of restoring the rule of the commodity, consciously regulating the class relation. This is not an untroubled solution because commodity fetishism can only flourish efficiently under conditions of a market which acts spontaneously. Racial discrimination is, therefore, necessarily contradictory. It divides the class, and in order to do so it intensifies the conflict, in a deflected white–black form. The problem is that the conflict is limited in time since the majority cannot be denied their rights forever. The black majority in this period, however, have been thoroughly politicized and though their demands are of a racial form they are in essence anti-capitalist. So, the capitalist class has bought time at the expense of an overthrow which is both inevitable and more far-reaching than any that might have occurred earlier. Nonetheless, they have bought time and that is what is most important.

We may sum up this part of the discussion by saying that racial discrimination in South Africa is one of the forms of the international division of the working class. It is similar but not identical with the divisions between migratory/immigrant workers and the indigenous majority or between the aristocracy of labour and the majority. The closest comparison is with the forms of racial discrimination in the United States. Its difference is that racial discrimination there is part of a general division of the class consequent on immigration, which is more important than the racial division itself in the control over the class. It would be possible to abolish racial discrimination in the United States but keep most blacks in the same position, through the operation of the ordinary effects of the reserve army of labour and control over labour. Indeed, to some degree this has already occurred. The same result would not easily happen in South Africa.

The reason for the difference between racial discrimination in South Africa and the more or less similar forms elsewhere lies in the nature of accumulation in the different societies. In South Africa, the surplus value extracted is partially re-apportioned among the white workers so creating a partial class antagonism between workers. The super-exploitation of the Irish workers did not necessarily mean a transfer of value between workers. The higher pay of the English workers could be regarded as pay at their value rather than below it and the difference could also lie more in the constancy of employment and in the nature of the jobs taken. Even the extra pay of the aristocracy of labour was limited in extent and even in time, which indeed allowed them to lead the militant strikes of the First World War. In a word, the pay of the privileged workers was not unambiguously a transfer from the superexploited section of workers.

In the case of South Africa there can be little doubt that there is such a transfer. The consequence, of course, is that the white workers both sell their labour power and so are workers and receive part of the surplus value and so are also part of capital. This would not be enough to argue that they are in a different position from those workers who are privileged in other countries if it were not for the fact that the white worker's relation to black workers is one of control over the labour of the non-whites as well.

If white workers control black workers, they are themselves controlled by white capital. The transfer of value argument is only clear if the workers receive a wage above their own contribution to value. There are two possible arguments in this regard. It may be contended that the aristocracy of labour had a higher wage because of the depression of wages of other workers, possibly in other countries. It does not follow that they received part of the surplus value, however, since they may only be placed in a better bargaining position. On the other hand, if workers receive a wage above their own contribution to value, so in effect costing the capitalist more than they are supplying, then they are unambiguously receiving a part of surplus value. It is not hard to argue that considerable sections of South African white workers were in this latter position because their actual contribution to labour time worked has been very limited in extent. If a white mine worker is in charge of a black worker, in a largely police role, then his contribution to value may indeed be negative. After all the elimination of racial discrimination would remove his job entirely.

Other white workers, engaged as skilled workers in industry, would be in a different position. If they are in charge of no blacks, their main reason for being placed in a group of capital's junior partners lies in their higher wages. They are privileged, in any case, in being skilled, as opposed to the nominally unskilled blacks. Still their position is not the same as those who are clearly receiving part of the surplus value. They are getting higher wages because the blacks receive lower wages. Then the question is whether profits are higher because of racial discrimination, the same or lower. If they are the same then the white workers are taking surplus value from black workers, if they are considerably higher then it is unlikely that there is a transfer of value but if profits are lower then a transfer must have taken place. There is little evidence that profits are lower than in other countries, though it is difficult to know the level of profits in the absence of discrimination.

The common assumption is that profits are higher and that the rate of profit is higher than that in many developed countries. Given the different levels of mechanization and so different organic compositions of capital, or capital/labour ratios, a higher rate of profit might not be due to lower labour costs. The other test is that of the rate of capital accumulation. The more rapid it is the higher the rate of profit underlying the accumulation. Again the result is not clear as periods of rapidity have been punctuated with low rates of accumulation.[18] There is, it would seem, no obvious evidence to state that the whole of the white labour force is receiving surplus value. It is argued below that the costs of racial discrimination are both high and clear to the capitalist class. It is then an open question as to whether a mythical non-racially discriminatory regime would have a higher rate of profit.

On the other hand, there can be no question but that there is a transfer of value from black workers to some, probably most, white workers. South African earnings, in the manufacturing sector, as a percentage of value added are actually above the level of major metropolitan powers at the present time. Even in 1970, the differences were marginal. Given the much wider income differences in mining it would be difficult to argue the cheap labour case for that sector.[19]

There may be some merit in arguing that the white workers are divided, as discussed above, between those who are receiving surplus value and those who are privileged but are not receiving such surplus value. This argument has been confirmed by the numbers of whites who joined the reserve army of labour in the post-1984 period and by the relative decline in the standard of living of sections of the whites. It has been this decline which has led to the emergence of far and still further right political organizations, who receive their support from these white workers. This discussion is taken further in the section on labour below.

What then is the role of racial discrimination in South African capitalism? The basis of capitalism is the expansion of value and value is congealed abstract labour. Hence in South Africa the expansion of value must take on a fractured form because abstract labour is itself torn apart. Why is abstract labour torn apart? Because the fundamental contradiction of capitalism, the increasing socialization of production, threatens to produce the ultimate negation of abstract labour, through the very strength provided by abstract labour. In other words, the workers become a collectivity to the degree to which they are interdependent and share a common form of exploitation. By becoming a collectivity they are able to overthrow the existing society. As a result, labour must either take power or be divided and in the South African form the division incorporates much of the complexity and subtlety of a declining capitalism. On the other hand, it also embraces the irrationality of a declining capitalism.

Whereas the mechanism and the material basis of the division has been analysed above, in summary form, no explanation has been provided for the nature of the actual division. It is not enough to state that there were blacks and whites, or that there was a history of antagonism. Brazil or the United States today do not legally discriminate against blacks, although racial oppression and forms of discrimination clearly exist. To stress the point again: there is no problem accounting for racialism as a doctrine. It is the promotion and extension of discrimination in favour of one colour group at the level of a whole economy that has to be explained.

In the metropolitan countries, the division of the working class between the aristocracy of labour and the rest has become an outworn form. The traditional division between those subject to the reserve army of labour and those who are not has been removed by the long period of growth since the Second World War. National divisions and sectoral divisions have become far more important. Whereas finance capital is international, the workers are patriotic, bound to the success of their own industries. It is this trade unionist defence of jobs, of industries and of countries that has provided the ideal division of the class, by craft, sector and country. At this point it cannot be argued that the division is an invention of the capitalist class. It is a necessary development of trade unionism as opposed to socialism in an epoch where the social democratic movement had progressively ceased to be revolutionary, both before and during the First World War. During and after the mid-1920s the nationalism of the USSR was instrumental in developing and extending nationalism in the working-class movement of all countries.

The point, however, is that the epoch is one of nationalism of a new kind, which has been widely exploited by the bourgeoisie, now that it has largely abandoned the doctrine itself. In fact, in South Africa, the division by colour is nothing but a particular form of the same general division the world over. It is the existence of social democracy and Stalinism that in the end permits the continued form of South African racial discrimination. Were nationalism to be seen to be the enemy of the worker, no worker of whatever hue could embrace it without knowing what he was doing.

The argument that it is not only class but also race or colour that is determinant in South Africa is put forward by Jack Simons as indicated above. He argues that the rigidities and feudal type controls are imposed on capitalism. As it is not just workers but also the bourgeoisie that is subject to these controls his argument has clear merit. The trouble is that such bourgeoisie as exists is very small among blacks, and even where it is larger, among Indians, they are not in production but in trade. In other words, blacks have effectively been prevented from entering the bourgeoisie. The small non-white bourgeoisie plays little if any role. Secondly, it has to be noted that while they are subject to the same laws, such as the Group Areas Act, they are accorded more respect and receive *de facto* exemption from some of the legal controls. Today, that has to be read in the past tense, as the powers that be in South Africa are desperately trying to form such a local black bourgeoisie. Discrimination between two groups of workers necessarily cannot stop at the workers, since otherwise the discriminated group could have its own employers, who might counteract that discrimination. The logic of class division by colour leads to colour division of all classes.

As the actual tiny size of any black bourgeoisie makes any argument based on simple colour division meaningless, the real argument rests on the discrimination against the so-called middle class. Once we exclude all those who are white collar workers we are just left with lawyers, doctors and intellectuals. The discrimination here again is not of the same kind. Clearly there is less question of job discrimination or fantastic wage ratios, although white professionals clearly have better salaries and opportunities. Such middle-class persons who are discriminated against are no worse off than the ordinary non-ambitious white in material terms, but the harshness of the discriminatory laws in transport, group areas, the curfew, the pass laws, and now identity cards, makes the discrimination all the more bitter. It is not surprising, therefore, that the present concessionary government measures are really aimed at them above all.

If the non-working-class component of the subordinate group is limited in size and strength, it does not mean that the argument for a colour division independent of class is wrong, although it is weakened. The fundamental question is that of the causation of the colour division within the economy. The argument hitherto provided is that racial discrimination is not independent of capitalism but on the contrary arises out of it, even if in its decline. Just as Hitler was a feature of capitalism and not feudalism, socialism or any other mode of production, so too racial discrimination arises out of the capitalist mode of production. The fact that a tiny section of the bourgeoisie is also affected does not show that capitalism has not given rise to discrimination, for after all Hitler jettisoned the Jewish bourgeoisie and no one dreamed of arguing that therefore anti-semitism was feudal.

On the other hand, racial discrimination does favour sections of white workers, but we have argued that they are part of an alliance with the capitalist class. In the end, the question reduces itself to the question of the primary source of movement. Is it colour *per se* or is it the nature of a declining capitalism to seek out methods of division of the working class, even at considerable cost to itself? Even though the elemental movement of the workers was the inspiration of the policy of rigid racial discrimination, it was the capitalist class which accepted it and used it.

On the other hand, it could be contended that colonialism is a different form of capitalism with discrimination against the indigenous inhabitants. This 'internal colonialism' then produces two sets of class structures. It is, however, not enough to refer to history. There has to be a driving force behind the maintenance of the so-called colonial features. The metropolitan powers did not prefer the policies of rigid and permanent racial discrimination which came to the fore. The settler discriminator is, however, a feature of colonies. The question is whether South Africa ought to be simply placed in the category of colonies, like Kenya or Rhodesia, now Zimbabwe. This question is discussed in some detail below. Briefly outlined, the argument is that there is only one class structure not two and that there is no clear evidence, as argued above, that there is an extra extraction of surplus value for the capitalist class.

The real reason why various observers have objected to the class argument is that race permeates not just the job but all aspects of everyday life. It therefore appears as if the division is a community division and not a class division. What these commentators, scholars and theorists have failed to understand is the nature of class itself. There cannot be a class unless there is a collectivity not just in consciousness but in a material form. It has already been argued that the effect of racial discrimination is to break up abstract labour to the extent that the labourers are politicized. They are, however, politicized in a particular way such that the collectivity becomes a non-class community. That, of course, is the great success of the policy of racial discrimination. That is also why no policy based on African nationalism can do more than overturn apartheid. In other words, what has happened in South Africa is that the working-class community has been replaced by a bastardized class/race community. What is that community?

Such a community does not arise out of itself. It is not a natural community. Workers in South Africa have a community but it has been so pressurized that it has taken on a specific form. It includes migratory labour, shanty towns, regular revolts and influx control. While these aspects are not uncommon for a working class, they are different from the experiences of the white workers. The Group Areas Act and Bantu Education are not just different from the acts governing whites, they also govern aspects of life which lie outside the factory and employment. They provide a still stronger sense of community, precisely because they are not involved, in the first instance, with the factory. Of course, all blacks whether rich or poor are governed by the same acts. Yet, the reason for these socio-economic forms, which control the lives of blacks, is what is crucial. It is not just to preserve the purity of the so-called white race. It is not just to preserve white rule. The purity of the so-called white race would be better kept if there were a complete separation of the legally denominated races. On the other hand, white rule, meaning white worker rule, might be better facilitated in a more backward, less industrial society, with complete nationalization. Strands of these two policies have exemplified themselves in government legislation and Nationalist Party thinking. Nonetheless, South Africa has continued to industrialize and integrate its population.

The point is that the deflection of the working-class community into an apparent nationalist form has occurred precisely because of the rupture in abstract labour. As a result, there is no working-class community but an apparently different entity, which, however, arises precisely from the potentiality of a united working class. The bastardized form which has so arisen is neither national nor racial. Still less does it have any historical roots in some other mode of production. It arises only from the movement towards the formation of a class, which has been effectively hijacked and turned into a pseudo-community form.

3

The Origins of Racialism and the Rise of Racial Discrimination

Racialism or the doctrine of the inherent inferiority of an ethnic group precedes discrimination, which can be defined here as embracing the forms of legal and customary protection of one ethnic group from socio-economic competition with another. Racialism served as the ideological justification of external primitive accumulation, which involved the extraction of surplus product from the inhabitants of other countries and of other modes of production. In the emergent and early phases of capitalism, capitalism relied on direct force and previous modes of production to extract and import a surplus from the world outside Western Europe. Its justification was provided by racialism. This, however, was originally merely an ideology to explain and compel acceptance of the brute force applied to other countries by the metropolitan European powers. Actual discrimination was not required since the Europeans were either in the business of extermination of whole groups of people or using labour power externally to the metropolis.

In South Africa, the early phase of capitalism led to the physical extinction of two of the ethnic groups who were originally there. It also involved competition for land and a limited demand for labour in agriculture. While South Africa remained agricultural the whites acquired all the land over time and subordinated the blacks as agricultural labourers, but then had a surplus of both black and white labour. As long as there was no industry, discrimination, as opposed to racial subordination, between white and black meant little. Both groups had the right to starve in the towns. Both groups were based on shifting systems of agriculture so that one or other group had to win in agricultural terms. In other words, it was not a question of competing workers or farmers so much as the defeat of one group by another. One author put it this way: 'the Cape before the Great Trek was not a society based primarily on racial distinctions despite the prevalence of prejudices and self-identification of the owners of property and possessors of privilege as white.'[20]

A peasant-based agriculture is based on the family and kinship group, even when of a non-industrial capitalist form, and hence requires the expulsion of those who are not of the right kin, or at least their subordination to the possessors of the land. Industrialized agriculture as is now present in South Africa requires only a manager and workers, with an absentee or otherwise landlord–capitalist. In the first instance, we have a case of dispossession, but in the second there is no room for large numbers on the land and competition among atomized workers for jobs comes into existence. Had South Africa remained agricultural this might well have happened. The initial phase was thus one of subordination and also the exclusion of those not required for labour.

Industry, however, was different as white capital could exploit any racial or colour group, on a mixed basis in large numbers. The increasingly impoverished peasants, white and black, flooded into the towns, where the issue was one of selling labour power on a competitive basis. On the farms the issue had been decided by force of arms but in the labour market black and white labour did not differ. The skill differences between a white peasant and a black peasant simply did not exist. The differences between white and black in industry arose out of the skill differences of imported white labour such as the Cornish tin miners. The British skilled labourer was, however, accustomed to the pay and control differentials normal to the aristocracy of labour in the United Kingdom and readily applied these differentials in South Africa. The mine managers preferred for the same reasons as in the United Kingdom to maintain the differentials over the unskilled labour. In South Africa there was the additional bonus that the less skilled workers could be distinguished by colour at a time when they were unused to industry and forms of trade unionism. The whites had the unions and the rest did not. This position, as it evolved in the towns and on the mines, was eminently favourable to capital as long as there was a real difference between the labour power of black and white and the proportion of white workers was relatively low.

It was not easy for the mine owners to obtain the masses of unskilled labour required for the gold and diamond mines as the peasants had no desire to immolate themselves. It was only through draconian measures passed by the state that the mine owners obtained their labour power. The pass laws, poll tax, migratory labour, and compound system of housing all owe their origin to the needs of the mining capitalists for cheap unskilled labour. There is, however, a difference between cheap unskilled labour, black or white, and a high rate of profit. The capitalists in this period accepted a distinction between black and white labour, which was at first connected with skill. There was, however, specific legal provision for the exclusion of blacks from certain jobs on the mines. They were not permitted to qualify for the necessary certificates of competence.[21]

This early exclusion of blacks from supervisory and skilled or semi-skilled jobs may be interpreted in two ways. In the first, the mine owners appear to be helpless before the white workers, whether in the old South African Republic, the British Crown Colony of the Transvaal or in the Union of South Africa. The laws so passed are the responsibility of the white workers or the Afrikaners. That the protection accorded to the white workers was due to their pressure cannot be doubted. The second explanation asks the question of the role of the mine owners. At first it paid the mine owners to protect the white workers because it ensured a loyal and stable workforce. The local managers would in any case have been racialist. Nonetheless, the number of jobs reserved legally for whites was limited and the colour bar operated both informally and through the use of skill barriers. The mine owners colluded in this form of racial differentiation as long as it paid them.

The second explanation is not the same as the first. In the article cited in note 21 below, it appears as if the essential villains are the Afrikaners using their control over the state apparatus.[22] In the second, the white workers are at first largely, though not exclusively, protected through skill barriers. The mine owners from this point of view colluded, as argued above, in introducing the pioneering forms of racial discrimination not because they wanted to maintain a protected white workforce but rather because they obtained a cheap black labour force and a stable environment.

The mine owners were seriously worried over the possibility of an influx of expensive white unskilled workers and hence colluded in preventing whites becoming unskilled workers, in order to keep wages low. The owners preferred to hold on to a flexible and fluid workforce, parts of which could replace one another when required. They were not inherently and rigidly discriminatory but rather more versatile in their response. They effectively maintained a doctrine of flexible discrimination. In this way, they had the best of all worlds.[23] They were nominally opposed to total discrimination, and in favour of education for skills. They protected the white workers but tried to limit their immunity; they gave shelter to the white worker in good times but turned on him when profits were low and the white worker could not defend himself. This early doctrine of flexible response to labour conditions was ideally suited to an industry which had a fixed price which could not be altered according to costs. The alternative would have been one of constantly revolutionizing the machinery in order to lower costs. This course was not taken.

Once, however, white workers became semi-skilled and unskilled workers on the mines and construction etc., the costs escalated and the capitalist class baulked at the loss of profits due to the relatively high wages paid to whites as opposed to blacks. At first they were able to employ cheaper Afrikaner workers to break strikes of the English craft unions. The latter discriminated against the Afrikaners but it was a losing battle, and the two groups coalesced. It is of fundamental importance to realize that the colour bar arose out of the nature of the craft union and the aristocracy of labour imported from the United Kingdom and not simply out of prejudice or some rotten Afrikaner nature, as some moralists have implied. It is not the triumph of reactionary ideas but of reactionary material interests. In the United Kingdom the concessions made by Disraeli led to an aristocracy of labour which was relatively highly paid and industrially militant. To ensure their privileges they were highly protective. In the United Kingdom and elsewhere this group was effectively discarded as too costly and counterproductive in the face of the changing nature of industry and the growing strength of all other workers. In South Africa, the British capitalist class also tried to limit their privileges and protectionism, in the period after the Boer War.

They tried to change the situation where whites were paid higher wages just because they were white. Strikes resulted and the political control of the country, resting on whites as against blacks, became less stable. This was the situation in the period after the stabilization following the Boer War. The mine owners were thus caught in a contradictory situation where they had conceded to relatively militant skilled white workers but they had also to concede to the less industrially militant unskilled white workers for political reasons. There was, however, a limit to their ability to concede given by their returns to capital. When profits turned down after the First World War they tried to cut costs in the obvious way by replacing expensive white workers with cheap black workers.

Black and white competed to sell their labour power in the market place and in the long run, without political intervention, there would have been a white skilled labour force with a mixed colour non-skilled labour force. In time, the differences in skill would have been eroded and the pay differential would have been reduced through the growth of industrial unions. This was the direction in which South Africa was tending in the terms of the market place and from the point of view of capital. The problem was that the very forces that capital had conjured up, the aristocracy of labour, combined with the kinship of peasantry and the anti-British capitalist Boer War history, served to rebel against capital itself. Racial discrimination had come of age. The discrimination practised against Irish workers in Britain, remarked on particularly by Marx, was now employed against blacks in South Africa.

Capital had begun by establishing legal controls over black labour while maintaining a labour aristocracy in the mines themselves as a means of economic control. It was able to manipulate the supply of labour to continue that division with its flexible response to white and black labour resistance, in such a way as to maximize its profits or minimize its losses. The problem was that labour was no longer controllable in the epoch of capitalist decline. The very aristocracy of labour turned on its masters in the metropolitan countries. Lenin was proved wrong in identifying the aristocracy of labour as the enemy within. In South Africa, too, the mine owners were no longer able to simply play off one section of workers against the other without major concessions.

4

The Historical Compromise

The fundamental turning point in South Africa came in 1922 when the white miners struck under the slogan of 'Workers of the world unite for a white South Africa'. The strike itself involved the Communist Party in a significant leadership role, while the workers themselves were both English and Afrikaans speaking. The strikers set up the Johannesburg Soviet taking power in their own name and utilizing effectively the example of the Russian Revolution. The Communist Party failed to demand that they join with the black workers and so stood in an ambiguous position. The white workers saw themselves as victims of the British mine owners who wanted to replace them with cheaper black workers. The latter stood aside in the struggle which involved the armed Afrikaner workers still fighting the Boer War but in the context of the class struggle. Smuts, an exceptionally gifted Afrikaner defector, bombed Johannesburg and at least 300 died, apart from those who were hanged. However, his government almost immediately conceded the real demands of the white workers by passing, in 1922, the Apprenticeship Act, which prevented black workers acquiring apprenticeships.

The white workers had a long history of fighting blacks in South Africa as well as struggling to avoid their own replacement by cheaper black workers (at least from 1907 onwards) but their own position was not fundamentally different from that of the black worker in education, standard of living or even culture. They may have had different religions and languages but they were both devoid of property of any kind, with a low standard of living and few prospects. They came as effectively illiterate or semi-literate peasants whose future was irrevocably bound to South Africa if they were Afrikaner or African. Their divisions were bound to disappear as white workers were ground down to the level of the black worker, just as Afrikaner and English workers formerly on opposite sides in the Boer War came to fight together against the mine owners.

There was no indigenous South African bourgeoisie and no South African middle class to support the British mine owners. A section of the Afrikaner farmers and the English petite bourgeoisie supported Smuts but they were both minorities in their own communities, mistrusted and fundamentally powerless without Britain. The only method of continuing to hold on to South Africa without conceding to the white workers was to send British troops, for an indigenous army could only be unreliable over time.

The context of the class struggle is all important: On the one hand, the British had conducted a costly imperialist war to maintain control over the mines, and had defeated the Afrikaners leaving a permanent legacy of great bitterness, while on the other the overthrow of capitalism was on the agenda. The Nationalist Party had supported the February revolution in Russia, it has to be remembered, and the Afrikaner workers were therefore not unaware of its sequel, which could be identified with the overthrow of their own imperialist overlord. The English workers had a trade union and often militant tradition. They too could not identify with the British capitalist class. The only alternative left was to crush the workers as workers but then concede to the white workers as whites rather than as workers. In effect, the capitalist class made the only retreat possible, at a time when the Russian Revolution was still alive and the European revolution was still on the agenda. Had the situation been quiescent in Britain, Europe and the Empire, the British could have simply crushed the revolt and taken the consequences as they emerged, but that was not the nature of the epoch.[24]

At the cost of repeating the point, it is not being argued that there was no racial discrimination before 1922. That would be absurd, but its nature was different. The land question and the restriction of land held by blacks to 11–13 per cent of the surface area was the imposition of the rules of conquest on the black tribes. The initial differences did indeed partly reflect differences in degree of skill and acceptance of labour discipline. Mine management preferred to employ white labour in supervisory and skilled positions. All this is fundamental. Nonetheless, the barriers were limited and relatively fluid, which meant breachable in principle and practice, as when the management found it to its advantage.

It is, of course, possible to argue that the real turning point came later, towards the end of the 1920s or in the early 1930s, when the organizations of both black and white workers had either been crushed or incorporated. This indeed is the argument of Innes and Plaut, who take the view that it was the destruction of black organizations by the government that made it impossible for the white workers to turn to them as a source of support against the employers. They cite figures to the effect that after the historic 1922 defeat, white wages declined and a deskilling process ensued. The white workers would, therefore, be expected to look for allies. By 1932, according to them, the Communist Party and ANC were impotent and the Industrial and Commercial Union (ICU), the black industrial union, had been destroyed. This destruction of the left was the result of victimization by the state. The white workers then had no allies and the minority who would have gone over to the blacks could not do so. This, of course, then opens up two further questions. Why was the state so powerful that it was able to pulverize the left? Why did the white workers never take a lead to organize and solidarize with black workers?[25]

In fact the Communist Party destroyed itself in South Africa as elsewhere, in the third period of the Comintern, through a combination of absurd policies and mass expulsions. The ICU decline has been traced to its peculiar formation, being neither a union nor a political party, which in the end succumbed to the control of one man and advice from liberals. The ANC never was much of a body other than for black professionals. They are right to point to the real defeat of the white workers but wrong to think that the course of history would have been different if not for the political action of the state.

History had conspired against the workers of South Africa. By 1923 the German revolution was defeated and Stalin was climbing the rungs of counter-revolution. A socialist alternative was soon impossible, once the global defeat was sealed. The Communist Party could provide neither leadership nor a refuge. On the other hand, substantial sections of white workers saw themselves protected, as a result of the strike. The white worker was protected from black competition, given employment with industrial expansion and provided with a ladder out of the working class. Innes and Plaut lay more stress on the ideological and political aspects of incorporation and repression. They are right that the incorporation of the white worker is not until the 1930s but the foundations were laid after 1922. It was not necessary for the ruling class to obtain a consensus among workers or even a majority to ensure that a trend was established. Nonetheless, their argument is infinitely preferable and superior to all the Gramsci/Althusserian so-called theorizing against which they were railing.[26]

The result was that the white skilled workers demanded and obtained limited forms of protection, but always in very partial ways. As long as there were relatively few white workers and the majority of blacks remained on the farms, whether white or black, the competition between black and white remained limited. This implied that the black farm workers or peasants on the white farms were clearly in an inferior position, but they were fundamentally no different from farm workers or peasants elsewhere in the third world. Indeed in a certain sense it was the Afrikaner capitalist farmers who first deserted their brethren in preferring the cheap labour of the African to the relatively more expensive labour of their relations or national group.

It was only when the workers of different races came to compete on a large scale that the possibility of legal, direct and openly discriminatory barriers could be erected. In other words, it was not previous history which introduced racial discrimination but rather it was the process of urbanization and industrialization itself. Put differently, before capital accumulation came to exist on the only basis on which it can maintain itself, abstract labour, differences between groups of various kinds maintained themselves and served as a means of discrimination, when required.

On the other hand, once modern capitalist production was established it required a fluid, mobile and homogeneous workforce. Capital necessarily broke all previous barriers of tribe, language, race, artisanal type skills etc. By so doing there was automatically created the potential of a united class, and indeed Afrikaner and African flocked to the towns with the same lack of skill and need to join the army of wage labourers. In principle, capital could have simply absorbed the workforce, provided that it was accumulating capital or growing, but it was not expanding during a period of declining gold prices, after the First World War.

In any case, the gold mine owners had no need to invest in non-existent industry in the colonies and so expand employment opportunities. Thus capital created the contradiction that on the one hand the process of capitalist differentiation among the Afrikaner peasantry drove the Afrikaners to the towns, creating the so-called poor whites, while on the other the new abstract labourers could not find employment, or if they could it was at a level below value. The African peasants found too that the restrictions on land imposed on them together with the poll tax drove them to work in the towns, but the employment opportunities were limited and the pay below their value of labour power as well.

The more desperate position of the African drove him to accept the conditions provided, not without protest or strikes. His position was fundamentally undermined by the migratory position in which he was placed. Had the industry involved not been gold the situation might have been very different. The reason was that mining, especially non-mechanized mining, needs abstract labour least of all industries.

Fully mechanized mining does indeed require the ordinary abstract labourer. In the absence of mechanization, however, the individual worker has a much a higher degree of individual responsibility. This in turn could only be maintained with adequate supervision or a solidly loyal hierarchy under conditions where the worker was totally alienated but able to determine his own rate of work in the absence of supervision. However, the other effect was that the nature of the work ensured that discipline and skill played little role. Hence workers could be employed who had never been subject to industrial discipline and had only agricultural skills. In other words the South African mining industry was ideally suited to migratory labour and stable separated supervisors. The effect was to place the black worker in an inherently more difficult position to maintain the value of his labour power.

Nonetheless, although the position of the worker in construction and mining, unless highly mechanized, is different from that of the industrial worker, the worker is still a worker and it remains the case that capital prefers to enforce uniformity on the worker to maximize production. The fact that it is more difficult and that it has to resort to forms of direct personal control is a contradiction which it has to accept.

There are, as can be seen, three stages in the development of the system of racial discrimination in South Africa. In the early capitalist period racial discrimination was only marginally present as racial conquest prevailed. Industry in the towns was too limited to require rules, while the peasants on the land were racially separated. Competition was competition for land, rather than between labour power. Intermarriage between different colours occurred and cohabitation was common. The result is that the so-called Coloured population and the Afrikaners derive from the same genetic background, even if the Afrikaners will not admit it.

(Slavery in South Africa was initially based on imported Indonesian labour under conditions where the slaves, who were political prisoners, were more cultured and skilled than their European owners. It remained non-plantation, non-mass slavery until abolished by the English in 1834. There was no pressure for mass enslavement to ensure production, as agricultural production, although capitalist, was based on a limited market, with a small surplus over subsistence.) The second stage began with the advent of mining, which required a mass labour force, but one easily adaptable to less homogeneity in the workforce. The third stage began when mining had to adapt to the world market and homogenize its workforce under stress, at the same time as manufacturing industry had shown its potential need for a homogeneous workforce.

In one facet South Africa may be regarded as merely a more obvious and objectionable aspect of a world-wide phenomenon. In the contemporary epoch finance capital became dominant and insisted on a ruthless international search for profits. As a result it is internationalist, in a manner that no other class has ever been. It will ignore all boundaries in its determination to make more money out of money. The source of surplus value, however, lies in production which cannot move in the same way, through a computer keyboard. It has to have a physical location with real workers. Whereas it might pay to shift locations from country to country to exploit poorer workers, it cannot be accomplished without real movement. As a result the relatively reformist and often reactionary labour movements become patriotic and protectionist instead of internationalist and socialist. The rate of profit is determined for the manufacturing capitalist through the movement of international capital and so by finance capital. As a result, management may solidarize with the workers against foreign competition. That workers should not be able to act in an internationalist manner, although industry and so labour is increasingly international, is also of the nature of the epoch and has much to do with the nationalism of the USSR and the proponents of socialism in one country.

The comparison with other countries is more apt when made with such as France with its racialist Communist Party, which has tried to compete with Fascists for the votes of anti-migrant French workers. The superexploited migrant workers of the European Community have to face the protectionist measures of their local counterparts. South Africa may be seen as the embodiment of the contradictions of world capitalism, from this perspective.

5
The Role of Capital

Racial Discrimination as the Regulator of Accumulation

It is now possible to see the contradictions operating on the process of accumulation which impelled the two groups of workers to both homogenize and compete. On the one hand the white workers were driven to the work in the towns in order to work at the same rates of pay ultimately as the black workers, while on the other they possessed the organizational strength to resist that tendency. The black workers did not have the organizational strength because of their objective position, although they could easily have joined together with the white workers in principle. In another context, the capitalist class could have simply ignored the white workers and employed only black workers, dividing the blacks between supervisors and supervised on the basis of pay or any other criterion to hand, such as language group. The problem was that the white workers were much too dangerous to ignore. At the same time, the black workers were wholly alienated, as a conquered group, who would revolt whenever the opportunity presented itself, even if it was not immediately. Thus the very process of capitalist accumulation in South Africa was threatened.

Not surprisingly there was only a limited industrialization until 1922 but, once the compromise was effected with the white workers, industrialization proceeded apace. It could do so because the barriers to accumulation described above were eliminated, but even then it was the Afrikaner controlled central administration which impelled the process of industrialization. The process was little different from that which proceeded anywhere using the Keynesian analysis. Significantly, British capital only invested in South Africa under the protection of state capital and in partnership with the emergent indigenous capitalist class. Racial discrimination from this point of view promoted capitalist accumulation because it divided the workforce, while in a peculiar way still ensuring the reduction to abstract labour in the long run. It performed the latter miracle by putting the white worker in supervisory, bureaucratic, military or artisan type positions.[27] As long as growth proceeded, the white worker could disappear as a manual worker, which has indeed occurred. Today some 60–70 per cent of Afrikaners work for the state or state-controlled enterprises, normally as white collar workers.

In a recent article, J. Abedian and J. Standish have shown the particular role of the state in absorbing 'poor whites'.[28] They estimate the nature of the replacement of blacks by whites, showing that whereas in 1920 there was a ratio of blacks to whites in manufacturing of 2.11, by 1935 it had dropped to 1.49 and then rose again to 1.73 in 1940 as industrialization proceeded. However, they also document the fact that the 'employment of poor whites was so much greater in the public sector than the private sector that there can be little doubt which sector contributed most to the reduction of unemployment.' This was accomplished by the dual process of protection of whites and an economic expansion, using the state sector which absorbed these unskilled and semi-skilled whites.

This industrialization process was effectively engineered by the need to expand production to secure stability, but it was made possible by the peculiar nature of South African production. In particular, this refers to the nature of gold as the money commodity which has acted as a countercyclical influence. In the depression years the gold price has gone up because the prices of all other goods went down. Similarly, at the start of the present general downturn in the early 1970s the gold price went up very considerably. In the first period the capital so obtained could be employed to invest in industry, while in the second it was used partly to raise wages and partly to mechanize. It has to be stressed, though, in contrast to most observers who ignore the point that, in the absence of a context where the investment had to take place, the profits would simply have gone back to the United Kingdom in the 1930s or been used to increase investment outside of Africa.

Gold has thus acted as the source of accumulation as well as the method of stability for the regime. In the latest period, in the 1980s, this mechanism temporarily broke down, with high interest rates making gold unattractive. Of course, internally many though not all gold mines continue to make high profits because the devaluation of the rand, which usually accompanies a low gold price, effectively raises the price of gold for the gold mines. In this latter case, however, the effect is to transfer the higher cost of imported goods to other sectors, which ultimately means the least protected workers, the black workers. The government has usually also altered tax rates to favour the mines, in adverse gold price circumstances. It did this for instance in 1989, when the maximum theoretical marginal tax rate was reduced from 70.5 per cent to 68.72 per cent. Since the revenue foregone, 31 million rand, had to be raised from somewhere, it can only mean that those who will pay the extra sales tax and higher excise duties must bear the burden.[29] In this case, it can only mean that the white workers, white-collar and blue-collar, will have to endure the austerity programme and the black workers will proportionately be harder hit, given their much lower incomes.

A genuine international rise in the gold price both raises profits of the gold mines and permits the government to make economic concessions to the blacks, and this will almost certainly happen again in the course of the current cycle. In 1986 the gold price began to rise again but it has only risen in relation to the dollar thus far. Nonetheless, one would expect that the gold price would eventually rise as interest rates dropped and the depression showed itself. Thus the stability obtained through incorporating the white workers was buttressed by the countercyclical nature of gold production, permitting the government and mine owners to use the extra money to ensure stability. It cannot, however, be too strongly stressed that such would not have been the case had there not been both a protective government and an industry in which investment could take place. Both government and industry were not the creation of the United Kingdom and its local class representatives.

The Nature of the South African Ruling Class

The Nationalist government introduced from 1948 onwards one of the most comprehensive systems of import control outside of Japan, which ensured permanent protection for local industries which had begun to develop with the industrial expansion promoted by the state before the war and fostered by it. The effect was to change the nature of the capitalist class in South Africa.[30] The old British mine owners were replaced by local firms, with strong international connections. Anglo-American, in spite of its name, is controlled by the South African Harry Oppenheimer, whose father came from Germany and became an Anglican in 1935 in order to ensure the neutrality of his products (diamonds) in an anti-semitic world.[31] English speaking capital in South Africa effectively became local capital, with strong links to Britain.

Although there is probably no large British company without investments in South Africa, the proportion of local funding for capital accumulation continuously rose to make external sources a relatively small proportion of annual investment. Afrikaner capital continuously increased its stake but it has never been more than a junior partner to this day. In mining, finance capital, and with such industrialists as Anton Rupert (tobacco), Afrikaner capital has become both large and influential but not dominant. However, the essential point is that the British ruling class clearly both accepted and probably preferred to reduce its stake in South Africa under conditions where it could no longer ensure stability. It reduced its stake in mining absolutely and relatively but could only increase its investments in manufacturing industry to a limited extent, since such an industry did not exist on any significant scale before the 1930s. Foreign investment in general has had to accept the policy of the Nationalist government, which was to indigenize production. Car production, uneconomic as it may be, was progressively localized over twenty or so years.

The policy of racial discrimination has had the most profound effects on capital accumulation in South Africa. It has increased the rate of capital accumulation, changed the nature of the capitalist class and prevented a fall in the rate of profit through state intervention utilizing the gold price. It is partly responsible, through the need to control labour, for the high level of concentration and centralization of capital in South Africa, a country where it is estimated that over half and more of all shares on the Johannesburg Stock Exchange – estimates vary – are ultimately controlled by one man, Oppenheimer. The mines have maintained a common labour recruiting organization since the early days of the gold and diamond mines, which naturally brought them into a cartel. At the same time the nature of the products required control over supply to ensure stability of price. Nonetheless, there is no other commodity like diamonds so perfectly controlled by the Oppenheimer cartel.

The strong state and centralized economic administration of South Africa provided an excellent environment for supporting the diamond cartel nationally and internationally. Nationally it maintains a special section of the police force dealing with so-called 'illegal diamond buying', so ensuring the Oppenheimer monopoly. Gold in its turn is assisted with state and para-statal bodies adjusting taxes and subsidies not to mention exchange rates which ensure profits. However, the control over foreign exchange combined with the lack of competition, and the support by the state of such a monopoly situation, has meant that there are limited opportunities within mining for expansion. Inevitably the profits of mining have gone to finance the development or acquisition of manufacturing industry in steel (Highveld), in chemicals (African Explosives and Chemical Industries), in cars (Sigma), all of which are major firms in the industry and all owned in whole or in part by Anglo-American, that is Oppenheimer. Profits have also gone overseas to a not inconsiderable extent but really in the form of South African subsidiaries, often to assist the South African base.

Thus the racially discriminatory form of accumulation has been basic in structuring the nature of the South African ruling class. It has become a highly concentrated class dominated by a few large firms, owned by well-known individuals. Barclays Bank was bought by Oppenheimer as well, giving him predominance in all spheres of the economy, except agriculture. In the end, Oppenheimer is the dominant individual of the class. The result is that the South African ruling class is not rent by divisions nor is it lacking in either tactics or strategy. The Afrikaner section is so much a junior partner that its role is more of a transmission belt than a maker of decisions. Thus General Mining, owned by Afrikaner capital, was virtually given over by Oppenheimer while he retained an important stake.

South African capital is not so much centralized and concentrated as peculiarly highly centralized as well as concentrated. The explanation, as we have tried to show, lies in the need to maintain a strong front to labour, the relative assistance provided for accumulation by the state, and the limited possibilities for investment in a mining industry with relatively poor mechanization.[32] All these aspects are themselves a consequence of the nature of racial discrimination in South Africa. The latter thus showed itself in the massive development of state industrial enterprises developed to ensure full employment for the whites. Railways, electricity, steel, fertilizer–chemical industry, and later, for security reasons, oil and so chemicals from coal, and hence many of the nationalized enterprises traditional in Europe since the war, have all been developed and expanded by the Afrikaner state.

Nationalized enterprises have been the main method of advancement for the Afrikaners to so-called middle-class positions, as well as assisting the development of Afrikaner private capital, much of which has become increasingly corrupt in the last few years. It is a liberal pipe-dream to believe that British capital would have otherwise developed South Africa. It did not do so in other countries of Africa, even in the presence of British settlers in (so-called) Central Africa , and the traditional reasons for antagonism to development in colonies remained operative. It is silly to deny this obvious fact just because the expansion of capital was assisted and carried out under the aegis of apartheid. The fact was that the white worker existed in an ambiguous position of being both an anti-colonial worker as well as a supervisor and later indeed exploiter of black workers.

Thus capital accumulation in South Africa has been regulated by racial discrimination, a term which has therefore to be understood as a special category of political economy and not just a particular politics of a particular group. It regulates profits, it assists the development of capital in particular directions, it forms the nature of that capital itself. It does all this in relation to the classical laws of political economy, which it does not abolish but rather seeks to contain and direct in particular ways, much as finance capital has done in the developed world or the welfare state has shaped accumulation in the present time.

The Role of Foreign Investment

The discussion above would give the wrong impression if it simply stated that there is an indigenous capitalist class. The links to the metropolitan capitalist countries remain strong, but in fact this is very largely a question of British investment. In 1982 around half of investment owned externally was British. Some 1,200 British companies are involved. Nonetheless, there continues to be a shift to internal control, partly because of pressure but also because British companies prefer to sell up where possible to reduce the risk. Historically, for Great Britain, investment in South Africa has been second to investment in the United States and that still remains the case. Around 11 billion pounds in 1982 would be not far from 14 per cent of British external investment. The figures are rough because valuation is dubious. What is clear is that the United Kingdom is far and away the major foreign investor in South Africa. The US held 30 per cent of the gold mining shares in 1979, and had less than half the value of British investment. South Africa is clearly marginal to the US in profit terms but not in the supply of certain kinds of raw materials and strategic goods.[33]

A contrary view on the importance of US investment has been made in a number of places. Thus one commentator, Raymond Lotta, speaks of the 'staggering' 'US involvement'. He finds that around $10.1 billion is invested in South Africa.[34] The South African Institute of Race Relations (SAIRR) gives a figure of 7.37 million rands for North and South American investment at the end of 1981, stating that 23 per cent of foreign investment in South Africa was from those countries.[35] It is true that the figures are very approximate and the devaluation of the rand will have altered dollar figures while it is also very true that US investment in British companies gives the US a further stake. Nonetheless the proportions remain very much the same and British investment in American companies also exists. The control of the investment, of course, rests with those who control the companies, not with minority shareholders. He also tries to argue that foreign investment was crucial for internal investment. The SAIRR, however, points out that the growth of external liabilities did not keep up with the growth of the gross national product from 1975 to 1981. This point he makes himself in another fashion. This only leaves the short period between post-1962 and 1975 as a period of capital inflow. He omits, however, to mention that a substantial portion of foreign investment flows just consists of reinvestment of retained profits. In fact in 1981–2 capital inflows from the US only accounted for a total of $100 million. By 1982 American holdings of gold shares had gone down to around one quarter, as compared with 30 per cent in 1979. The same source (SAIRR) points to the substantial divestment that only became possible with the liberalization of exchange controls. Because of the gyrations of the exchange rates the total figures mean little and cannot easily be compared between years, but the proportions are clear.

Lotta cites the importance of Citibank as the fourth biggest bank in South Africa. As the first two, Barclays and Standard, were both British and held on to the dominating stake in banking, fourth place is only overtaking the weak presence of Afrikaner capital. Both British banks recently decided to dilute their holdings in their subsidiaries to under 50 per cent, in order to get out of a risky situation. By autumn 1986 Barclays sold out to Anglo-American Corporation. Thus indigenous capital continues to increase in a way that it has done for half a century.

The continuing disinvestment of American firms may make the argument academic. On the other hand, the disinvestment of firms like IBM has been largely formal in that the ownership changed but the sourcing of the items from IBM has not. The point, however, of this argument is that there has been a general overestimation of the role of American capital in South Africa.[36] Indeed, the stronger attitude of the US Congress towards South Africa has a lot to do with the absence of a substantial pro-South African industrial or financial lobby.

The real axis is clearly that of indigenous capital in coalition with British capital. The other countries play a secondary role, though not in trade terms. South African industrial expansion was largely financed from internal resources. If the very large outflow of profits and dividends is considered, then it is clear that South Africa could declare a moratorium on all payments to external creditors and holders of investments and have no further internal investment problems. This is clearly impossible for political economic reasons, but it does give the relative importance of local capital which is expanding rather than contracting. Already in the 1970s, Charles Harvey pointed out that foreign investment could not be used as a lever against South Africa because it constituted less than 20 per cent of total new investment. He concluded that 'The cessation of new investment from abroad would not therefore stop the economy growing – indeed the economy grew extremely rapidly in the period 1959–65 when the net figure for foreign investment was negative.'[37]

To illustrate the above, South Africa had balance of payments on current account surpluses of around 6–7 billion rand in 1985, 1986 and 1987, but only around 1 billion in 1988. If not for the international pressure which is compelling it to expand in order to reduce internal tension, it would have a very considerable balance of payments surplus. It has to be added, for instance, that the surplus on foreign trade was 13.5 billion rand in 1985, but with a negative invisibles account of over 6 billion, only 7 billion rand was surplus on current account. If it is added that estimates put the amount leaving South Africa at some 10 billion in 1985, the net extraction of surplus value from South Africa can be seen to have been close to 16 billion rand or 8 billion dollars at present exchange rates. In fact both because of undercounting and because of the artificial exchange rate the real outflow is much higher. The net loss both on service payments and capital outflow for the past decade has been considerable.[38]

The 24 billion dollar debt now owed was effectively incurred because of the pressure placed on South Africa by the International Monetary Fund (IMF) and so the United States to liberalize its financial markets at a time when South Africa was in recession. The effect was a considerable outflow of funds from the country, intensifying the need for foreign borrowing. This was then made even worse by the demand for foreign loans by firms who preferred the low external interest rates to the very high internal ones. In principle there is no great risk in lending to South Africa even now, as a *Financial Times* leader of the 4th April 1986 made clear even after the Southern African foreign crisis debt began. Few countries could sustain an outflow of 16 billion rands out of a gross domestic product of 119 billion rands, maintain negative interest rates, and attempt to expand internal production. Indeed, by the beginning of 1989 South Africa had reduced its foreign indebtedness to $21.5 billion. Only because of the decline of the dollar has the indebtedness not fully reflected the officially estimated capital loss of around $25 billion, over the past four years.[39] The main reason for the plug being pulled on South Africa, then, is not financial, but rather that capital does not want a future working-class revolution on its hands.

There is a further problem: where does one put South Africa on the scale of development? In terms of the nature of industry, where it has its own aerospace, motor, machinery, metal using and arms industries it is not underdeveloped. Nonetheless it remains dependent for technological advance and for finance capital upon the major developed countries. It is the most developed country in Africa and is usually compared with Australia and Canada. Today that probably underestimates the relative independence of development of South Africa. It is larger in population terms and can in fact draw on the resources and labour of the surrounding region, which makes it considerably more advantaged. Nonetheless it is stunted by the small internal market for durable consumer goods, low productivity and the very low African standard of living.

The Costs of Apartheid to the Capitalist Class

In spite of all the foregoing the capitalist class has never liked apartheid. It may be as well at this point to make the distinction between apartheid and racial discrimination. Apartheid must be regarded as the particular policy followed by the Nationalist Party of South Africa, which involves both the use of direct force to control the blacks and the elimination of all blacks from any form of competition with whites. Hence it incorporates hostility to a black middle class, job reservation for white workers and strict separation of the so-called races by location. None of these aspects were liked by the bourgeoisie, which preferred, as argued above, a more flexible form of racial discrimination.

The capitalist class has accepted the more rigid form of racial discrimination from 1922 onwards, it has used it, but it has always found itself in conflict with its regulation. Even if the dominance of South African capital over its former rivals, and the predominance of a few capitals, has much to do with the existence of apartheid, the beneficiaries have constantly railed against the way in which the laws of the market have been constrained or, as we have said, accumulation has been regulated. The fundamental reason lies in the need for capital to operate freely without constraint, unless it is to operate inefficiently in relation to its own criteria. Apartheid does not necessarily reduce labour costs, strange as it may seem to those accustomed to decades of simplistic Stalinist propaganda. It does mean wages below the value of labour power for blacks, but it also functions to raise wages of whites far above their value. Taxation in order to keep whites in employment also serves to reduce profits, while the whole state apparatus has to be much larger in order to ensure security. This too has to be paid for either through taxes on profits or through inflation, which creates a special problem for gold mines with a fixed external price.

Of course, a reasonable compromise has been functioning all along but it remains a constant source of friction to the capitalist class that in principle their profits would be higher in the absence of apartheid. Bourgeois economists never tire of pointing out how apartheid restricts their beloved market. They are right, though they never point out how much the existence of that market owes to apartheid. The capitalist class, though less than happy, were quite prepared to accept this relatively costly situation until it threatened their existence and their profits, with its natural termination.

It has to be added that the costs of apartheid are not limited to questions of higher taxation on business and extra payment to whites. The limitation on the market, owing to the low salaries paid to the majority of the workers, has meant that the traditional consumer durables such as cars, even if internally made, have a restricted demand and consequently the whole collection of industries which have gone along with it has been similarly stunted in size. Investment has had to go into other industries or into greater centralization of capital. The effect of having cheap black labour and expensive white labour which has been effectively protected from dismissal has meant that mechanization has been more limited than otherwise would have been the case. In turn, the demand for machinery has been more limited and so the engineering industry has been skewed. This applies mainly to the more labour intensive industries such as the mines and construction. It is interesting to note that South Africa is now going for the electrification of black residential housing, which will not add much to total electricity production but will increase demand for consumer durables.[40]

More central manufacturing industries found in time, particularly in the 1970s, that the 'shortage' of skilled labour, as well as the instabilities associated with unskilled labour, made capital intensive investment highly attractive. This has led to high levels of mechanization coexisting with the previous low levels of mechanization in the same industry. The result is that levels of unemployment have tended to rise rapidly. As South Africa has not got computer industries or a machine-tool industry to compete with Japan or Germany it must import modern equipment, which not only strains the balance of payments but also creates demand outside the country not inside it. A home market of 36 million would not permit internationally competitive industry unless it was, like Taiwan, internationally orientated. That, however, has been ruled out, so that the natural market in Africa cannot be reached. South Africa has a dominating presence in Southern Africa and beyond but its possible imperialist extractive role is actually limited by the abhorrent nature of apartheid.

The third aspect of cost to the capitalist class has been the absence of sufficient skilled labour to perform the tasks required in industry. Modern industry requires, Braverman notwithstanding, a flexible, mentally agile workforce able to cope with rapid technological change even if their individual tasks are not very demanding. This requires more than the few school years blacks in fact receive in the main. There are now several hundreds of thousands of black white collar workers and tens of thousands of professionals but the economy requires many more. There is an immediate limitation on expansion with the absence of the requisite labour, but there is a far more damaging effect, which deserves a separate discussion.

Both black and white labour cannot and do not function in industry in the form required. They both work below their potential to a greater degree than is normal even in a country like the United Kingdom.

Blacks are badly paid, operate in a highly disciplined not to say nineteenth century regime and so perform as badly as they can get away with. Worse, they are paid below their value and so are often in poor health, worried, drunk, and they die at an early age. At the same time the migratory labour system ensures that skills have to be constantly relearned and the unfortunate labourers have to live in suboptimal conditions from the point of view of production. Whites are relatively too well paid and are largely in employment for life and so have even less incentive to learn or be more than lazy. The result is certainly less than optimal from the point of view of the employer. Even if he has no strikes at all he has a real labour problem which is insoluble. The natural solution, as in the USSR, is to go for maximum computerization both to replace workers and to control those remaining and that is now the overall tendency.

It can thus be seen that while the capitalist class could accept racial discrimination as the least worst alternative, it caused substantial costs and in the shape of cost problems also directed the nature of accumulation in a way not preferred. Even if the capitalist class has much to be grateful for in the present regime, it has always preferred to find its own market type solutions. The fact that in a dying capitalism it could not have developed South Africa or at most would have had a South American style regime of underdevelopment and consequent dictatorship cannot alter the objective contradictions in which they find themselves. They accepted the solution presented to them as the one which would maintain their continued existence and they have willingly paid the price as long as the goods could be provided. Today and particularly with the labour unrest of the 1970s the deal is no longer worth it from their viewpoint, but they have no obvious solution. The question of the solution will be discussed later.

It may be objected correctly that still the rate of profit for US investors in 1982 was around 12 per cent internally but 18 per cent for investments in South Africa. The problem with this type of statistic is that it reveals very little except that the price of South African shares are marked down to include a risk element. To work out the real rate of profit or the real rate of surplus value is a massive job, further complicated by the obvious fact that the modes of hiding surplus value are different in the different countries. It further does not tell us what the rate of profit would be in the absence of apartheid, since it may be even higher.

Capital and the South African State

The South African state, as may now be clear, is certainly different and separated from the bourgeoisie, but only within limits. The Oppenheimer interests are obviously not as strong as the British state in 1922, but their internal influence is enormous. It would be wrong to conclude that if the Oppenheimer family had been able to remove the government they would have done so. It has not been in their interests to oppose the government to the point of removal. On the contrary, the accession of the Nationalist Party to government followed the abortive mine strike of 1946 and there is much to recommend the view that a strong government was in the interests of the mine owners. It would appear that attempts at white opposition of a more militant kind were dealt with quietly but firmly.[41]

The use of words beloved of Althusserians and followers of Poulantzas like overdetermination or relative autonomy not to speak of the phrase 'in the last instance' tell little of the reality of the relationship of the ruling class to the state. Clearly the problem in South Africa is that the state has personnel different in ethnic composition as well as position in the social structure from the ruling class in South Africa. The bureaucracy, army and secret police are Afrikaans speaking and come from families of white workers or white farmers. Furthermore, these people have used their political position to acquire wealth and change their position within the class structure. The South African ruling class, however, is closely allied with British capital and hence international capital, as has been amply demonstrated by the support South Africa has received from the British government and British companies over sanctions. The controls needed over South Africa can be exerted internationally if required. The mild sanctions imposed are really a reminder to the state personnel that they are disposable if required. More important was the way the international banks pulled the plug on the economy and plunged the government into a crisis, from which it is now emerging with reforms and a radically new determination to save capitalism by building a black bourgeoisie.

The problem for Anglo-American is that they can certainly replace the government with a more reform minded party but such a party would not have the zeal to die for a cause, which ultimately is that of capitalism. The costs of using the Afrikaners amount to little when compared with the risks of replacing them. Today there is an army which will defend the present social order to the last man. Stability is guaranteed for a time even if at a price. The problem is that the alternative is increasingly a socialist-minded black working class and that the present order is making sure that no other form of opposition is possible. To ensure that stability is maintained beyond five or ten years the alternative has to be in place today and that is why the Afrikaners are indispensable even now to the bourgeoisie. They have contempt for the boorish Afrikaners but the latter have their uses for the time being.

In other words, the South African state is manned by personnel who have their own interests, and the bourgeoisie has to accommodate to them but only as long as they serve the purpose of the state itself: to ensure the stability of the capitalist order. As long as the instruments of repression are effective the price can be paid, but once they become counterproductive new personnel with new instruments are necessary. Engels pointed out many years ago that the bourgeoisie had lost the stomach for ruling. He was referring to Bismarck and the way in which the bourgeois parties accepted semi-aristocratic government to achieve their ends.

As capitalism has declined the capitalist class has had to make concessions to the working class and find new allies in its determination to maintain capital. In Germany in the 1930s, for instance, it allied itself destructively with the petite bourgeoisie. It may be asked whether the German ruling class was sensible of their own interests or were simply upstaged, but this is to ignore the reality of the time and the results of Fascism. Europe was still threatened at the time with the possibility of revolution and Hitler made an extra-ordinarily good job of wiping out the left, incidentally assisting the consolidation of Stalin's power, and, on an international scale, setting the scene for an unbelievable re-invigoration of capitalism. It is true that a section of German capital was wiped out and that the war destroyed yet more capital, but at a time when capital was threatened in its very existence, this was a price which had to be paid.

There is, to put the matter clearly, no last instance. The state always acts to preserve the social order but it cannot always do it without some damage to the interests of the capitalist class. This takes two forms: individual members being sacrificed – a normal feature of capitalism given its brutal competitive spirit – and major concessions to other classes. As capitalism declines the latter becomes more important, leading to lower profits rather than no profits and to the acceptance of the diminution of the sphere of capital itself in order to preserve the remainder.

In South Africa, the British capitalist class accepted a local agent which they despised and which involved a shift of capital to the 'colonial' territory. They thereby retained the system and found a vastly expanded sphere of operation at the cost of sharing surplus value with a former section of the working class and petite bourgeoisie. It is a complex relation but it is one in which the state never fails to ensure the immediate survival of capitalism.

The often quoted example of the frustrated attempt by the mine owners to establish permanent family housing for blacks in the 1950s does not show that the state and the mines were at loggerheads. After all, the refusal to permit permanent black residents ensured the absence of a black community such as Soweto for a longer period of time and the state was acting in the interests of security. The mines, on the other hand, were exploring the possibility of alternative methods of control than the ones then in existence. Anglo-American was caught by its need to maintain the existing security arrangements and the long term survival of the system, which required the introduction of a welfare state. The latter, however, cannot be introduced piecemeal, for the racial discriminatory state and system are indeed a particular form of capitalism and as such cannot be changed gradually. It required a determined and public commitment to abandon and oppose the whole existence of apartheid.

It may well be the case that the bourgeoisie of South Africa and of the United Kingdom have lost both capital and profits over time. It may also be the case that the bourgeoisie would like, indeed would dearly like, to change the system today. On the other hand the state will not permit them to do so. Does the bourgeoisie not then control the state? In the first place, any change in South Africa has to take account of the realities of the political situation. In other words, simple movement to abolish all racial discrimination would cause a white revolt, while opening the door to a black socialist movement. The white revolt could have been accepted provided alternative personnel existed to staff the apparatus of the state. That is not the case in South Africa as no black army could be expected to suppress a working-class insurrection. Thus the bourgeoisie has to accept the white, largely Afrikaner, army. Such acceptance entails concessions to the whites, particularly its white and blue collar components of the workforce, to permit the timing of change to be left to a less painful future.

This leads to the, already stated, conclusion that the bourgeoisie has to force change from outside the national state onto that state rather than directly controlling it. This involves pressure inside South Africa and outside South Africa. The trade sanctions campaign is certainly not part of the strategy of the bourgeoisie and constitutes only a minor pin-prick for the regime. The capital boycott is, however, of their making. The banks pulled the plug on South Africa and have given it clear terms. The withdrawal of American firms has been largely cosmetic, involving, as it does, continuing supply of the necessary goods from the metropolitan country. The acquisition of Barclays Bank by the Oppenheimer empire in the autumn of 1986 is only a shift of capital from the United Kingdom to the local bourgeoisie. In spite of the anti-apartheid campaign the fact of the matter is that no metropolitan bank would remain in South Africa if it did not get more out of South Africa than it invested in it. The mere presence of two British banks in South Africa rather than indigenous banks has meant little, other than proof of the importance of imperial interest in and over South Africa. The utility of South Africa to imperial interests, which today are of a finance capital form, rather than a colonial form, is clearly considerable but it has to be very carefully masked and balanced against the other forces at work. The movement of imperial capital, even if only in a nominal form, out of South Africa is a clear signal to the state to conform or suffer the consequences. Capital has thus the best of all worlds.

Though approving of the present strategy in South Africa, capital does not have to have any hand in the actions of the state in its devastating and brutal white terror campaign. It can safely criticize the government for not proceeding fast enough, knowing full well that the government is proceeding as fast as is politically expedient. It can attack the government's measures against individuals knowing that these measures have ensured the stability of the regime. It can attack the whole restrictive political process knowing that it will not change for some time. Capital wants change, but only change that will ensure its own long term survival, where long term means ten to 20 years. Hence it must keep up the pressure for change while ensuring that the change occurs in a measured way.

The Debate on the Role of Capital in South Africa

The apparent differences between the state and capital have led to considerable confusion particularly on the left. John Saul illustrates this confusion on the left when he tries to argue that capital has not always been against apartheid by seeing different fractions with different interests. He describes an Anglo-American director who wants to put the case for capitalism to blacks as a farsighted capitalist, as opposed, no doubt, to a near-sighted capitalist, who would simply retain capitalism. Saul then speaks of the absence of a consensus among capitalists. He is, therefore, arguing that the capitalist class is divided and therefore cannot act. That capital works through a consensus, however, is a fantastic concept belonging to a world never hitherto seen. Capital has acted either because its dominant interests require action or because its collective interest needs measures to be taken. In the latter case, the logic of the requirements imposes itself. There is no point, however, in engaging in any theoretical debate since it is not believable that South African capital should require a consensus when one man or one empire almost own the country. It is quite clear that the views of the dominant owner of capital, Oppenheimer, are determining for capital in South Africa. What is not clear to him, or to anyone, is the strategy to maintain capitalism in that country without racial discrimination. That he is opposed to it matters little for he has to ensure that he has capital, albeit at a low rate of profit, rather than no capital. Hence his empire has to oppose radical change, rapid movement to dismantle apartheid, and, as Saul points out, even one man one vote. 'Senior managers at Main Street like to compare their lot to that of a filling in a sandwich, caught between black radicals and white reactionaries. This is how they explain the group's inability to use its massive commercial power to push the government faster down the road of righteousness.'[42]

This does not mean that the South African state is simply acting on its own, as he says, or that the South African state has a better understanding of the needs of capital than capital itself. It only means that capital today has to be very careful in its actions in case it loses everything, and hence it is best served by proceeding cautiously in promoting black capitalism and gaoling a large number of militants. The apartheid state has never been the state that the capitalist class preferred but it cannot be dismantled overnight. The absurdities of the state can either be temporarily accepted or, if they become insupportable, rejected, ultimately through international action.

It is interesting that Saul ends up in the same camp as Lipton, in seeing capital as lacking any programme. The state then appears autonomous, guaranteeing capital's interest because capital has no programme of its own. Why the state should so act or receive such wisdom is entirely unclear.

Certainly by international standards the defeat in South Africa at the present time is awful but nowhere near the catastrophe of the Paris Commune, to take one example. The reason has something to do with world opinion, but that was in no way evident in relation to the atrocious massacres of Indonesia, over a million people, or for that matter the large numbers arrested and killed in Chile. It has far more to do with the fact that the state is not controlled by its apparatus alone and that the bourgeoisie would not be served through the liquidation of its workforce.

The argument developed here is one which argues that capital has been well served by flexible discrimination but has had to accept more rigid forms to ensure its own stability. The state that has come into being is one which has served their interests albeit in a form that they did not like, though accepted. The relative independence of the state when there are equally powerful warring classes is not in evidence in South Africa. The South African state is outspokenly anti-communist and stands for private enterprise. No state today can exist through force alone and the South African state has mass white support.

Althusserianism and Marxist Theory

Discussion in South Africa, on the left, has been dominated by Althusserian concepts. The fundamental critique of the Althusserians, which is implicitly made in this article, is that they use political concepts, when they ought to be using 'value' concepts. Both obviously have to be employed and it is clear, for instance, that this article is arguing that South Africa can only be understood in the context of a political decision to divide the workers. That argument, however, is made by reference to the nature of value itself, through the categories of abstract labour and superexploitation.

Wolpe rails against his fellow Althusserians for the arch crimes of 'reductionism' and 'economism'.[43] If he and they had not been trapped in the entrails of a dying Stalinism, they might have noted that the simplistic view of the relations between base and super-structure maintained by J.V. Stalin never had anything to do with Marxism, of any kind. The structuralist opposition, which they have adopted, by a curious inversion retains the original Stalinism.

The essence of the Stalinist approach was in fact structuralist since it looked at relations between structures: production relations, legal rights of ownership, forces of production, and superstructures. Two points are being made. Firstly, Stalin saw these latter categories as structures. A production relation, for instance, was defined in terms of the class structure in production. Secondly, he concentrated on a static relationship between groups. He divorced political economy, in other words, from social relations.

An anti-Stalinist view, however, looks at the extraction of the surplus product and hence at the form and control of the surplus product. From this starting point the laws are derived and linked into the social relationships. There is, therefore, both movement, derived from the laws, and conscious change derived from the intertwined movement of the categories of the society and class struggle. The laws themselves derive their dynamic from the contradictions between the form of the surplus product and human needs. Quite obviously, Stalin could not speak of the extraction of the surplus product because the Soviet population would then have been enabled to discuss Stalin's appropriation of the surplus product. Instead he insisted on formal structures like ownership, which were obscure at best and derived from the very superstructure which he considered to be determined by the base. The word 'determine', in turn, is a dynamic concept and never meant a one to one change in, for instance, ideology, propelled by some demand of the economy.

It is being argued that it is the causes of change which lie in the base, and in that sense the superstructure is 'determined'. Cause, in turn, has to be interpreted in the sense of a driving cause rather than efficient or empirical causation. Only those bound within Stalinism would argue that in art, for instance, new modes of perception did not have their own validity. Two points are important here. Firstly, different entities are never reducible to their component parts. So art is not economics and cannot be explained by some law in economics. Secondly, every aspect of an entity has its own efficient causation.

Changes in the form of the surplus product determine the direction of the superstructure. For instance, the value form obviously leads to the invention of legal conceptions of ownership in order to maintain legal forms of control over the surplus product. A specific division of the surplus product which leads to particular forms of capital accumulation can lead in turn to specific legal and political forms to enforce that particular division. Such is the case in South Africa, as argued above. The political forms, in turn, are used to maintain the specific relation. Although we can say that the politics is determining the economics at any one point, in the sense that the state is enforcing obedience to the status quo, yet the state is doing so precisely because the particular form of extraction of the surplus product has to be defended. It is not a question of 'determination in the last instance' or 'relative autonomy' but of a continuous underlying imperative which provides both the direction and the limits of any aspect of the superstructure.

That does not mean, for instance, that art must be pro-capitalist or anti-capitalist but that the changing nature of the social relations and so the form of surplus extraction will be crucial to any understanding of that art. The artist could have any political point of view or no point of view. It is not a question of politics, which has its own dimension. Nor does it follow that anyone could trace the interrelations between art and the society in the same period. It is only argued that the underlying laws of the political economy are fundamental for an understanding of aspects of the superstructure. They do not provide any guide to the internal workings of that aspect itself except in so far as they condition it.

Art is an extreme case in that its own laws of development are not known and Marxists certainly know very little of it. The obvious fact that South African literature is dominated by the question of racial discrimination, even when it is not the subject of the book, and that the different sections of the society have written very different literature, even if they agree on politics, makes the point. I have taken the case of art because it is the strongest case for the Althusserians. When we turn to the state, the structuralist argument looks weaker. The simplistic view of the state as capital itself, enshrined in the doctrine of state monopoly capital, propagated by the USSR and its ideological allies, could never be Marxist. One form cannot be reduced to another. That was the problem with the general Stalinist view of Fascism and consequently with the absurd attitude that South Africa is Fascist. Fascism is not a development of state monopoly capital. It was a specific historical phenomenon, which has to be understood in its context.

The crucial categories which the Althusserians fail to use are those of Stalinism, and declining capitalism. Thus no understanding of Hitler is possible without comprehending his symbiosis with Stalin and the aid occasioned the Nazi party by the Communist Party. Yet, not unnaturally, Althusserians and their derivative Poulantzians refuse to discuss the question. That Communist Parties, throughout the world, have supported their local states, on specific occasions, is well known. Much has been made of anti-communism but the under-pinning of anti-communism, in the horrendous nature of the police states and former police states in the East, is overlooked. The point is that the success of the modern state has had much to do with Stalinism. The very use of the apparatus of repression under capitalism has been underpinned by its extreme function in the USSR, Eastern Europe etc. This point has become clearer with the changes in Eastern Europe in 1989–90. One party states became more difficult to sustain throughout the world and 'Western ideology' lost much of its rationale.

In the second place, a declining capitalism is not the same as a rising one. Engels, long ago, made the point that the bourgeoisie no longer has the stomach for governing. A declining capitalism has special political problems. It has to deal with the power of the working class, under conditions when its own strength is declining. It has, therefore, to make concessions over government. It has conceded universal suffrage, and consequently will rarely get the ideal government for itself. The state, however, is not the government. In the United Kingdom it has long been obvious that the police, army and bureaucracy nominally and in reality answer to the monarchy, and not to the government. In South Africa the state apparatus has no monarchy to which it can owe allegiance. The Governor-General, who served the same purpose in South Africa, has been abolished. In Australia, however, the Governor-General's dismissal of the Whitlam government showed where the real power lies. The Afrikaners, who man the relevant institutions in South Africa, are certainly not socialist today so that there is no problem of the maintenance of capitalism. There is, however, a problem for the state in managing a transition to a less racialist society. Has the state apparatus then been transferred away from the capitalist class?

The answer, however, lies in the nature of the South African capitalist class. We have argued that it is international. It has a state that is also international. Precisely because that is the case, the local state understands its own position. It will, therefore, under most circumstances obey instructions. Indeed, in the last few years, the Afrikaner bureaucracy, police and army have overseen a certain transition away from so-called petty apartheid. If they do not act as required, the international bourgeoisie can use financial pressure, as it has been doing over the past few years. If that, in turn, does not work, they can always use the United Nations and apply force.

Finally, a declining capitalism must accept that, in certain circumstances, it will not be able to utilize the state apparatus to defend capitalism. After all, that is what happened in Russia during 1917. As the society crumbles so does the state apparatus. The ordinary soldiers, civil servants and policemen join their class and assist in the overthrow of the society. In South Africa, on the other hand, the bourgeoisie has conceded control to a section of the petite bourgeoisie under pressure from the workers, who have manned the state apparatus. In other words, a declining capitalism may keep the state apparatus intact but it cannot either fully control the government or the personnel in the state apparatus. It has to live in an uncertain world and make do pragmatically with the material it finds.

This does not mean that the state is an arena of struggle, as the Althusserians put it, because the state itself is unchangeable under capitalism. Under socialism it would, of course, wither away, but in the transition period it would have to be completely recast to serve workers' interests. Put differently, either the state serves the interests of the ruling class or it collapses. There is no intermediate situation.

6
Labour in South Africa

The Nature of White Labour in South Africa

There has been considerable discussion around the question of the relation of black to white labour in South Africa. This is not an historical book so that the question considered will only be a more detailed discussion of the earlier question of the relation of black to white labour. Can the white workers be regarded as extractors of surplus value? The relation of white to black wages has varied over time, reaching the extreme in mining of 21 to one in 1970, but six to one in manufacturing. If it is considered that real black wages, in mining, had not altered since 1911, though white wages had, of course, gone up considerably, it is clear that there is a strong case that many white workers do not simply constitute an aristocracy of labour but are in fact junior partners in exploitation.

On the mines, white workers were less than 10 per cent of those employed and have tended to go down in numbers rather than up. These extreme figures make the point succinctly. Black/white wage ratios of ten to one were the norm for mining for some time after the war, while since 1971 black wages have gained considerably. Even so, 1982 ratios of 5.5 to one on the mines and 4.4 to one in manufacturing and construction do not permit a view that white workers are not also exploiters. In fact, there are some 400, 000 whites in production, who are largely artisans, supervisors etc. in charge of other workers. The remaining 1.5 million whites in employment are administrators, white collar workers and distributive workers. Even by 1960 Jack Simons was arguing that since 60 per cent of the white urban population were in non-manual occupations and 82 per cent of the manual workers were skilled, there was a 'trend towards a bourgeoisie'.

Since many of these are in the unproductive sector they necessarily receive surplus value from the productive sector and, given their relatively high wages in relation to blacks, they must also be held to be at the least in an ambiguous position. In the absence of apartheid, white pay would clearly go down, even given the most optimistic growth and productivity assumptions.

This description provides a more detailed survey to underpin the initial argument of this book that the white workers have to be divided into sectors. Some do indeed receive surplus value from the black workers, others do not but are in a controlling position in relation to black workers and a relatively small proportion are simply privileged workers. It is this latter category which looks like being jettisoned by the regime.

The political importance of such an analysis is straightforward. White workers, white collar or blue collar, can only be opposed to black rule, since their standard of living would be bound to fall. In the first instance, it would involve them paying a higher level of taxation in order to finance state housing, roads, health and education for the blacks. They must suffer a drop in their standard of living for this reason alone. There is no way around this conclusion. Even with a considerable rise in production and in productivity, white salaries will have to fall. Whether this occurs through inflation, taxation or a reduction in paid income is irrelevant. The capitalist class is not likely to reduce its overall rate of surplus value to protect the white worker when he has become a source of instability rather than a junior partner. The white workers, using the term, worker, to mean wage-earners, all those who sell their labour power, can only oppose change of a genuine or radical kind. Cosmetic changes, or ones which do not affect real income and conditions, will be accepted by the white collar group, who are less directly threatened. The professionals and business executives are not threatened except by the possibility of a socialist revolution and so are pushing very hard for real changes.

The Afrikaners today are no longer farmers or even blue collar workers, although a minority are of course in these occupations. The majority have moved up the scale to white collar jobs, particularly in the state apparatus, and they can certainly accept limited change, but anything else will entail considerable sacrifices from them. In a genuine non-racial republic many of them would lose their jobs to the several hundred thousand well educated black, Indian and coloured persons, to use the categories of the South African state. The English speaking section (40 per cent of the whites) has less to lose since they tend to have more professionals, administrators, and business executives. They also could leave the country more easily than the more indigenous Afrikaners. In a socialist republic, the English would have more to lose of course.

We may conclude, therefore, that the white workers are to be divided into four sections. The skilled white collar workers, as for instance engineers, draughtsman, tax collectors, the routine white collar workers, as clerks in the state administration, the skilled workers and the semi-skilled workers. It is the last three categories who have most to fear from any change. They are not homogeneous in that those in charge of black workers without any skill other than those of policemen are clearly receiving surplus value, while those who are genuinely skilled workers may not be in charge of anyone and may not be regarded as receiving surplus value. The semi-skilled white manual workers, who are generally Afrikaans speaking, are bound to forego their privileges, and they have every chance of joining the reserve army of labour. The routine white collar labour can only go the same way with the difference that there is a greater time gap involved. These are also occupations generally occupied by women in most developed economies. Clerks and distributive workers are already increasingly non-white jobs, and the civil service jobs of this kind must also cease to be the province of whites alone.

The conscious attitude of white workers is well known. A March 1985 survey of white worker attitudes to upward social mobility of blacks found that their views were discriminatory and based on their own perception of losing their 'protected position'. They wanted reservation of jobs for whites and were opposed to equal training for blacks. 44 per cent even opposed equal pay for equal work. The survey was of 603 white artisans in Pretoria.[44] This is, of course, only to be expected. The white workers constitute, therefore, the conscious bulwark of the opposition to dismantling racial discrimination.

Black Labour in South Africa: Workers or Peasants?

South Africa is a modern capitalist country with contemporary industry, though not in any way on a par with the United Kingdom or the United States. From the 1930s onwards the left has been bedevilled by a second problem, other than the question of the origins of apartheid. That involves the nature of the African exploited and oppressed masses. Are they workers or peasants or both? A glance at the statistics will show that while there are very few black non-workers, even today officially only 38 per cent are urbanized. Some six and a half million blacks are in work, outside of the Transkei, Venda, Ciskei, Bophuthatswana area, out of a total population of 24 million or so, including those areas. The figures are given a spurious legitimacy by their detailed nature although the actual black figures are certainly greater, because it does not pay many blacks to have themselves down on registers of any kind. Nonetheless the point is still illustrative of the problems. Furthermore, some 1.3 million blacks are economically active in the so-called independent republics, and a similar number in the 'homelands'. This produces a figure of one third of the economically active population in the area formerly known as the reserves, who are effectively eking out a difficult existence largely on the land. However, the *de facto* position is that there is a rotation of jobs between the enforced periods in the old 'reserves' and work in the economy entitled the white areas. Furthermore, the actual income and nature of work involved relegate it very much to a tertiary role.

The essential question has been greatly simplified by the continuing mechanization of the farms. Some one million blacks were estimated to be farm workers, that is working on white farms. The numbers are decreasing as the old labour tenant system was abolished. Formerly, blacks would work on white farms for pittances but eke out a living from a plot which they cultivated. They were paid but they could only subsist as long as they used their own plot to supplement their income. Naturally, they preferred to go to the towns but the pass laws prevented them. Hence some Marxists concluded that between the reserves and the white farms the majority of blacks were peasants, or in the words of the *de facto* theoretician of the major Trotskyist faction: the peasant question was the alpha and omega of the struggle in South Africa.[45] Since blacks were tied to agriculture, to particular farms or reserves and possessed, though seldom owned, plots it seemed a reasonable view in the 1930s.

Burlak, the leader of the Spark group of Trotskyists, held that only manufacturing industry was the basis of modern capitalism and he was clearly right that mining and construction are industries that are thousands of years old. Marx does indeed make this point, in the *Grundrisse*, that these industries have a separate history and different work process. That much is true. The problem is that these industries in South Africa are capitalist even if at one time poorly mechanized. Farming too was effectively capitalist. The farms were assisted by the state to accumulate capital and consequently become more and more concentrated. Mechanization proceeded relatively fast even when workers had their own plots. On the white farms the blacks were effectively selling their labour power, albeit at a very depressed rate. Blacks in the reserves increasingly found they could obtain very little income from agriculture so that the families really existed on the basis of wage labour supplemented by the tiny amounts wrung out of the poor land on which they existed. Thus Burlak's argument looked dubious both because it did not see the obvious trend towards proletarianization but also because he was probably wrong even when he wrote in the 1930s. The other Trotskyist group, those with the *Workers Voice* journal, took issue with Burlak therefore on the grounds that he ignored the importance of the growing black working class.

The importance of the discussion was that Burlak was led to argue effectively that the form of the struggle had to be against racial discrimination alone and not for socialism. His side was buttressed by letters from Trotsky which appeared to take this view. Trotsky really did not have much to say about a part of the world of which he clearly knew little, but in his letter to Burlak he stressed that they had to maintain a firm line on racialism. Little can really be concluded from such a statement as it is consistent with a struggle for socialism under banners calling for the abolition of racialism. Nonetheless, it was taken to prove that the nature of the struggle in South Africa was bourgeois democratic. Hence the major Trotskyist movement took this line. The Unity Movement, which has had very considerable influence in South Africa, therefore adopted a ten point programme which was fundamentally bourgeois democratic.

The Nature of Fractured Abstract Labour

In this section the concept of abstract labour is further explored. We may summarize the initial discussion on abstract labour as defining the concept in terms of the social homogenization of labour. Its consequence is that a fluid, competitive and flexible workforce is created and maintained.

Turning to South Africa, we find that the nature of racial discrimination is such that there is only a limited common form of labour between white labour and black labour. The same was not true of the British aristocracy of labour, so clearly demonstrated when the skilled workers led strikes during the First World War. In South Africa, the whites work under different conditions at different intensities for different periods of time. There are different reserve armies of labour. This fracturing of abstract labour goes beyond the white/black division as it has led to major differences between the sectors of the economy, between parts of the country and between firms.

The nature of labour under the circumstances of South Africa, thus, has its own theoretical meaning. In particular, it has been pointed out that the mining industry found it possible to accept less homogeneity because of its relatively backward nature, that is its low level of mechanization. Under these circumstances labour could actually be divided in a manner which made labour more individualized and so less homogeneous. In other words, the mines did not have abstract labour. The cost of production was of necessity higher than it would have been under other conditions, though cost of production here only refers to quantity of labour time. Transfer of value to a section of capital which has extra labour time above that socially necessary, which would be the case, implies both that other sections of South African capital were deprived of resources and that the buyers of gold paid above the value of the metal. The mine owners then extracted a rent from society, which was possible because of the exceptional importance of gold mining to the society and the special nature of mining to the extraordinary depths required to extract gold. They very quickly cartelized themselves.

It is thus clear that in the absence of other pressures the mine industry would have prevented the emergence of industry itself. It could not then be metropolitan capital or mining capital which initiated the industrialization of the country.

A further consequence of the fracturing of abstract labour was the indeterminateness of the cost of production in labour time terms. This arose because the workers (both black and white for opposite reasons) could not be homogenized between the major sectors of the economy, agriculture, manufacturing and mining. Agriculture had insufficient mechanization for a long time and far too many workers in relation to the work required. It thus extracted its traditional rent from society. Apart from prices of food, inputs into agriculture have been subsidized. Agriculture and the mines were thus in a very similar position, though not identical in relation to industry. Manufacturing industry required genuine abstract labour and in fact imposed a greater degree of homogeneity than in the other two sectors.

The consequence for the three sectors of their lack of abstract labour has been a competition and antagonism unusual in most capitalist countries. The relations between industry and the mines have been relatively good for two reasons. In the first place, the state promoted the industrialization and the mines simply accepted it as a *fait accompli*. In the second place, major sections of industry were duly integrated into holding companies with mines as their major holding. Nonetheless, spokesmen for manufacturing industry are often noticeably more liberal in their attitudes. This is not really an indication of greater humanism so much as the expression of the reality of modern industry, that it cannot function well without a fluid workforce able to move geographically and vertically. The latter is the condition for the existence of abstract labour itself.

A still further consequence of the division of abstract labour and so of non-homogeneous labour is the gross inefficiency of the system. In fact, this involves more than just extra costs, for the effect of workers of different colours working at different rates, at different times, in different industries makes control over the workers much more difficult other than through political measures. The worker is not subordinated to the machine in the same manner as in the developed countries, whether black or white. The worker, equally, is politicized and not simply subject to an all pervasive commodity fetishism both in direct domination or as ideological propaganda. In this sense the workers of South Africa are more advanced than the workers of the developed countries. In other words, the usual controls exercised in a developed capitalism have been replaced by a form of direct political control. The workers are politicized, though held back by the community basis of struggle. Put differently, they are a class in potentiality struggling to bring that potentiality into a phenomenal form. The real conflict in South Africa is between capital and labour but the contradiction in the formation of abstract labour has created all the tension in reality as well as in theory.

This last point needs to be elaborated. The foundation of the class in reality lies in its existence in the form of abstract labour. In so far as this is limited the class itself has a lower potentiality for existence as a class, that is as a collectivity. It can display its action in various other forms, as an urban community for instance, but it has a barrier in its formation. Clearly, there is no possibility of unity between white and black workers but there are material problems in uniting mine workers with industrial workers and agricultural workers. There are problems in uniting the reserve army of labour with those in employment given the differences in location. There are always problems in overcoming the divisions of the class since it is in and through those divisions that capitalism survives at all. The peculiarity of South Africa is in the nature of those divisions. The increasing mechanization of South Africa has been destroying the fragmentation of the labour force. The demands of value production have begun to enforce the existence of abstract labour to an ever greater degree.

This argument does not lead to the view that it is necessary to wait until every worker is similarly subordinated to the machine in production, a prospect which is absurd. When the process of politicization combines with the socialization of labour, and so the common relation of all workers to production in however limited a form, a revolutionary process will be under way. The very actions taken to preserve the status quo, the limitation of abstract labour, limits the nature of value in the country and, as discussed, commodity fetishism. The capitalist system is then seen politically and not as an eternal economic formation. At first, the form of labour appears to be simply a racial form but it is soon realized that the subjection to the machine and hence to capital is no better under black capital and black foremen than under white capital and Afrikaner foremen.

Hence the permanent and particular contradiction of South Africa is its permanent and increasing politicization. Hence too the race on the part of the capitalist class to find a method of re-introducing market forms into parts of the economy which have lacked them. It has demanded and got a privatization programme. It has demanded and got the abolition of the pass laws and so the removal of the controls over labour mobility. In fact, however, neither the pass laws nor the privatization programme have gone more than a very small step in the direction needed.

It is worthwhile concluding the political economy section by summarizing the effects of the fracturing of abstract labour on the political economy of South Africa. On the one hand, it has maintained the stability of the country by preventing the emergence of class actions while on the other it has led to communitarian forms which have challenged the state though not the system. It has politicized the population in a dangerous manner though not sufficiently to lead to the overthrow of the social system. In this respect, of course, the global rise of nationalism, ably inspired and assisted by Stalinism, has played a crucial role. The contradiction of the system is that it must industrialize and so increase the power of the workers, who ultimately must become increasingly socialized and so anti-capitalist. To prevent this eventuality they have maintained the fracturing of abstract labour in spite of the costs to their profits and the increasing concentration of capital which has become necessary to centralize an otherwise divided economy.

7
Political Movements and Policies

The primary political movement for the last 30 to 40 years has been the Communist Party and its close ally the ANC. Other organizations have been important and the ANC/CP still may not have majority support among blacks in South Africa but it remains true that it has played a crucial role in the country's political evolution. It may be argued that its role has been entirely negative. The purpose of this section is to demonstrate the political origins of the present non-socialist, communitarian, and nationalist line.

The Communist Party and its Vicissitudes

The South African Communist Party had already adopted a bourgeois democratic programme from the time of the 6th Congress of the Comintern in 1928 where Bukharin put forward the slogan of the Black Republic.[46] The party then expelled both those in favour of a socialist black republic and those who wished to continue to operate among the white workers. The Communist Party was ineffective during the 1930s and by 1940 it had only 280 members.[47] The Trotskyists, particularly Max Gordon, played a not inconsiderable role in the unions.[48]

The divisions among other theorists on the nature of South African society showed itself also in the South African Communist Party, though it appeared a decade later in the 1940s. The party was divided between a more right wing, Browderite wing, which later took power when they went underground in 1950, and a more socialist grouping. (Browder was the post-war leader of the American Communist Party who wanted to dissolve the Communist Party and merge it with 'progressive forces'. In keeping with the popular fronts of the war years, he saw a gradual change in capitalism itself.) The socialist grouping played the more prominent role in the later forties almost by default, as the right wing of the party was under attack with the development of the Cold War. Obviously, the harder line adopted by Stalin helped the more militant wing of the party. However, those in favour of making the struggle in South Africa a socialist one never really had much of a hope given the close links between the Communist Party and the USSR.

The latter, under the direction of I. I. Potekhin, put forward a nationalist solution to South Africa, one in which the different language groups received different parts of South Africa. Potekhin was the head of the Africa Institute in Moscow and was only advocating what already existed in the USSR.[49] In the context of South Africa it could only mean a movement based on nationalism and one moreover which conformed quite closely in principle to the doctrine of apartheid in its purist form. This proposal has recently re-surfaced in the USSR, in a more modern form.

The Communist Party thus came to put forward the view that South Africa was essentially a colony whose settlers perpetuated the colonial status of the blacks and hence there was something called internal colonialism being maintained in South Africa. Thus the struggle was also bourgeois democratic. In Soviet terms it was National Democratic. The academic and theoretical expression of this viewpoint is in the works of Harold Wolpe, as already indicated.

The South African Communist Party, when driven underground in 1950, shifted to the right, with the reformed Browderite faction in control. The formerly left line which prevailed in the 1945–50 period under the influence of H. J. Simons, but also in a period of Stalinist cold war was dropped in favour of nationalism. In 1948, a prominent member of the Communist Party declared that they were a class party and should not tail end the nationalists since their purpose was to lead all the people of South Africa to socialism.[50] Yet again, the Communist Party, at its last legal congress in 1950, declared in its report, 'On all sides the national and racial differences are being emphasized, and the realities of the class divisions are being obscured.'[51]

The 1950 Suppression of Communism Act outlawed communism 'as interpreted by Lenin or Trotsky'. The Communist Party officially dissolved itself, and one of the two men (M. Harmel) who voted against dissolution then played a crucial role in building up the party. The ANC, contrary to much contemporary propaganda, had been a largely middle-class organization with a limited influence. Dr. Xuma, the head of the ANC in the 1940s until 1949, was noted for his moderation and was opposed by members of the ANC Youth League, such as Nelson Mandela and Oliver Tambo. Yet both the ANC itself and the Youth League at the time, pre-1950, were not noted for their support of workers.[52] Indeed, the more militant Youth League, as Baruch Hirson notes, even called on the help of 'spiritual forces' to assist the mineworkers in their 1946 strike.[53] The Simons similarly argue that Congress was no more than radical liberals with no strategy. As they point out: 'Communists and its own left-wing urged the Congress to adopt a grass roots organisation based on local branches and cells.'[54] In short the Communist Party, banned in 1950, reconstituted itself underground with a new platform for national liberation as a first stage in a two-stage struggle, and proceeded to work through the African National Congress, in which they played a determining role.[55]

The ANC now acquired a programme, the Freedom Charter, which has a series of non-racialist democratic demands but also includes the nationalization of the mines, something which the leadership originally resisted. It is impossible to imagine a non-racialist South Africa with white owners of the mines superexploiting the black workers. It is possible to have the mines under private black ownership but with a high level of mechanization and so with many fewer workers, all much better paid. However, it is difficult to imagine the mines easily embarking on such a programme except under public ownership. Apart from the mines the demands are essentially slogans for bourgeois democracy. Naturally, there are no references to genuine workers' control, self-management etc.

The issue of the mines became an immediate issue when Mandela emerged from prison in early 1990. He reiterated the need to nationalize them, but this was greatly qualified by Joe Slovo, who made it clear that both a private sector and international capital were necessary. A socialist society, he reiterated, was not on the agenda.[56]

Returning to this ideological history of the Communist Party, passive resistance became the political tactic in conformity with the line from Khrushchev who was pushing peaceful coexistence. This amazing strategy, of peaceful change, was ended when the ANC was outflanked by more militant former members who objected to what they saw as the lack of democracy as well as to those in control. These African militants formed the Pan Africanist Congress (PAC), but their initial success was overtaken by their own fragmentation and lack of resources. The ANC did not have the same problem. It simply rooted out dissidents, or worse. It had the resources provided by allied countries, including both the Soviet bloc and Scandinavia. It had to outflank in its turn the PAC, which it did by first embarking on a bombing campaign and then going for armed struggle. Since it was well endowed it became the premier nationalist group outside the country.

The Communist Party is, of course, normally regarded by Government propaganda as the inspirer and controller of the ANC. The truth of that proposition is complex. The ANC has become the only mass organization with a national and international presence. Arguably it does not have a democratic mass structure but it has a mass appeal, not held by other organizations of whatever kind. The result is that both its members and those of the United Democratic Front (UDF), largely controlled by the ANC, are far from being Communists, Stalinists or Marxists. Since the CP has largely organized itself around nationalism and anti-racialism, its members and the members of its sister organizations know very little Marxism. They are rather closer to a radical nationalism, in support of the USSR.

Hence, the capitalist countries and the banks are not wrong to deal with the ANC. Although the CP may be crucial, it is almost certain that a bourgeois democratic South Africa would lead to a break up of the ANC and of the CP itself. Paradoxically, the nationalist, bourgeois democratic form is largely if not entirely due to the Communist Party. Of course it is open to question whether the introduction of a classically Stalinist form of control would not prevent dissidence. The CP is caught by its own bourgeois democracy which would be guaranteed by the capitalist powers. A multi-party democracy would quickly arise while the increasing degree of popular grassroots control in the townships and in due course in the factories as well could not be easily suppressed. Today the emergence of more democratic forms in the USSR probably means that the Communist Party must accept a competitive multi-party electoral process.

The nationalist line of the CP has meant that it has neglected the working class, which organized outside of the CP and so ANC. Nonetheless, it is clear that the new federation, the Congress of South African Trade Unions (COSATU), has quickly fallen under ANC/CP leadership. Control from above cannot operate when the working class establishes genuinely democratic forms such as workers' councils or workers' control over factories. The result is that the working-class struggle will necessarily go beyond the bounds of the ANC, making yet another reason why the line of the CP has to be nationalist and for concessions to private capital.

Reading of the Soviet material on South Africa, produced by the Africa Institute, makes it clear that the USSR will not fight the US over South Africa. They accept that it is an American sphere of influence, in which the regime must fall and concessions would have to be made to the African population, though in the form of a National Democracy. The coded terms imply that the USSR is looking to a government which remained economically capitalist and so Western orientated but politically was friendly to the USSR. This has been the Soviet line for the last two decades. Gorbachev has simply removed all ambiguity. That solution is not really on offer and hence the relative stability of South Africa amidst its obvious instability.

Gorbachev's policy is one of international withdrawal in order to deal with the internal economic crisis. The USSR has, therefore, told the South African Communist Party to come to a deal.[57] That indeed is what must now happen. In part, this is the result of the evolution of Communist Parties. They no longer have a policy, other than the introduction of the market in countries where they are in power. It is no longer clear what Communist Parties do when they take power.

In part, however, the change of line is a result of the dependent attitude of the South African Communist Party towards the USSR. It is one of the last of the Stalinist parties. It has the unique distinction of justifying the Soviet invasion of Czechoslovakia before it happened. Its leader of that time, Michael Harmel, showed his allegiance, with an article in *Pravda* in 1969.[58] In the latest period, the South African Communist Party has undergone a traumatic experience, with all its cherished beliefs in Stalin and the wonders of the USSR questioned by the USSR itself. Not unsurprisingly it has published an attack on the Gorbachev leadership by Gus Hall, the leader of the US Communist Party.[59] That it should demonstrate its independence, at last, in such a manner, is an occasion for humour but not belief. This was shown by its subsequent turnaround, when it expressed full support for Gorbachev.[60]

In the South African context, this can only mean that the Communist Party will increasingly adopt the policy of the United States, that of building up a black middle class, but under anti-racialist and socialist slogans. It is even more interesting that the Soviet regime is now dealing directly with South Africa. That they have maintained contacts over their common economic interests in gold and diamonds has been clear, but that they should find a forum in which to negotiate, as they did, in March 1989, in London, is a natural evolution of a subterranean trend.[61]

Workers' Demands and Capitalist Solutions

The Pass Laws and their Replacement

The key demand of the African population for many years, and so of the working class, was for the abolition of the pass laws. In the few years before 1986, roughly 200,000 persons per year were arrested under these laws. The Minister of Law and Order estimated that 17 million Africans had been arrested during the period that the pass laws were in force.[62] They played a crucial role in the control of the workforce in South Africa, given the importance of migratory labour, the supply of labour to the uncompetitive sectors, and the need to maintain security.

The abolition of the pass laws, with the Abolition of Influx Control Act of 1986, did not mean that all controls over labour were abolished. It is, therefore, instructive to observe the necessary functions of the pass laws and the nature of their replacement.[63]

The pass laws fulfilled the function of controlling the reserve army of labour, in the absence of a poor law or welfare state, enforced the labour contracts in the towns, ensured that the workers did not need any welfare benefits and so reduced taxation on the whites. In the absence of the pass laws it would not be easy to control the black townships. They performed, therefore, the central political–economic function in the system of racial discrimination.

The government's response to the inflow of black workers has been its policy of 'orderly urbanization'. Blacks who are nominally attached to the so-called homelands are regarded as aliens and hence deportable and controllable. The rest are controlled through the various acts which provide for supervision over the district of residence as well as through the laws against squatting and slums.[64] Above all, the lack of accommodation makes movement to the towns self-limiting under conditions of very high rates of unemployment.[65]

Contrary to the views of those who talk of a two stage programme, there are probably no Africans in South Africa who are not workers at some stage in their lives. The mine workers go from 'reserves' or Bantustans to mines or farms or industry in rotation. Agriculture in the reserves or homelands simply cannot support the population and has not been able to do so for this century. As indicated above this situation has only got worse over time. As a result of poll taxes Africans have been forced to go the towns to work. On the other hand, they could be deported from the towns or compelled to work in the mines or agriculture through the use of the pass laws. The pass laws, then, were central in maintaining the system of migratory labour.

South African agriculture has now been so mechanized in the last few years that the labour force on many farms has been reduced to ten per cent of its previous level. The former allocation of plots to farm workers has been greatly diminished so that the proportion and the nature of the farm workers has changed in the direction of wage labour. Under one third of the African workforce is now officially employed in agriculture, some ten per cent on the mines and the rest in industry and services. Under these conditions, agriculture can be supplied with workers through the high reserve army of labour.

The mines have employed non-South African labour for a long time now. In addition, the relatively higher rates of pay combined with a very high reserve army of labour can also serve to maintain the supply of labour to the mines.

The actual number of those in employment is relatively low but that is in part because of the high rate of expansion of the African population (around 3 per cent) producing a large number of persons below working age. It is also, however, a reflection of the true high rate of unemployment with the unemployed being shunted off to the homelands or reserves. The 8–9 million economically active, out of 26 million Africans, include 4 million or more persons who cannot find jobs.[66] The exact number of unemployed is a political question with the government producing figures nearer to 20 per cent and private estimates making it much higher. One 1988 estimate gave a figure as high as 5.5–6.1 million.[67] With low to negative growth rates, high rates of inflation and high interest rates it is only to be expected that unemployment would be very high.

The question, however, is not the exact size of the unemployed population but how this mode of control, shunting the unemployed out of the cities, can be replaced, under conditions where there is no peasantry and there is a permanently high rate of unemployment. On the above figures it would appear that close to half the economically active African population are unemployed, though it is argued that a substantial proportion are involved in subsistence agriculture and the informal economy.

It is true that in the last decade the rise in rates of pay on the mines, decrease in numbers on the farms and increased housing facilities have made the system more flexible. Numbers arrested under the pass laws had declined substantially from the 700,000 in the peak year of 1969. In addition, the mine owners as well as manufacturing capitalists prefer a stable labour force, which does not revolt or strike too often. On the other hand, migratory labour always had the advantage for the mines that the workers were easily controllable, housed in policed compounds and constantly having to renew their residence in the reserves or go to other countries. The independence of the neighbouring countries, together with the increased militancy of the local workers, has compelled change. Wages and conditions in the mines had to improve, but in the absence of the pass laws the rate of absenteeism, labour turnover and labour militancy must all increase.

The solution appears to lie with a series of political economic realities. In the first place, the very high unemployment might serve a similar function to the pass laws in controlling labour. After the initial period of the re-establishment of control over the population, the pressure of competition will force the newly urbanized workers to accept employers' conditions. It has to be noted that the position of the reserve army of labour in the second half of the 1980s was very different from its position in the 1950s and 1960s. The decline of agricultural employment and the rapid rise of the numbers in the workforce can only tend to force wage levels downwards.

On the other hand, the level of unionization is now estimated to be some 35 per cent of workers, which is far higher than before legalization of unions and strikes. This provides the workers with considerable strength. Today, however, the mine owners encourage black unions as a means of control over the workers, whereas they opposed them for a long period after the war. Indeed the National Union of Mineworkers might be seen as being encouraged by Anglo-American.

Harry Oppenheimer declared his opposition to the pass laws, so that one might think that the mines never needed them, conveniently forgetting they were the original source of the pass laws. It is true that wages in the mining industry have increased since 1969, but they are still not competitive with industry. Indeed, mine worker wages have actually fallen further behind in the last two decades. The mines claim an increase of 'partially skilled' black cash wages by 285 per cent since 1971. On the other hand, average wages in manufacturing industry had increased by 352 per cent in the period 1975–1987. The ratio of cash wages between the sectors is of the order of two or three to one. Farms also still need labour at low levels of pay.

On the other hand, the mines can be comparatively unworried as long as they can import most of their labour from abroad or from the 'homelands'. The import of labour from the so-called homelands, whether nominally independent or not, implies the existence of an extensive reserve army of labour. The division of the African workforce between those in permanent employment in the towns and those who are not is certainly an important mode of control open to the regime. Nonetheless, what is crucial is the replacement of labour by machinery, so changing the nature of employment in the mines and reducing the numbers required. This also enables the mines to dispense with the otiose white workers. As a result, the mines may find that costs not only do not increase but can actually decline.[68] This assumes the elimination of the white workers, with their hugely expensive wage bill. A slimmed down and more efficient workforce may not suffer all the problems mentioned above, as pay and conditions would be sufficiently attractive especially if long-term unemployment is the alternative.

There can be no doubt, furthermore, that welfare benefits will have to be provided for a section of the blacks, and that this will mean increased taxation. The army and police might have to step up their activities. It is instructive to note that the recent budgets and in particular that of 1989 have made provision for increased expenditure on the police and armed forces and taxation has increased.[69]

The African population desperately lacks housing facilities, with many people being forced to live in shanty towns. With the abolition of pass controls the situation has worsened. This, of course, indicates the need for a crash housing programme. This indeed is the overall programme of the so-called reform but the government still insists on self-financing of the housing constructed. The solution is clear. The relatively skilled blacks will obtain the housing but the rest will not. Housing can then be used as a mode of control.

The Group Areas Act still applies so that the government can still keep blacks out of parts of the country where there is no scheduled space, or very little. The abolition of the pass laws may mean fewer arrests under the nominal pass laws, but the question of arrest for contravening curfew, labour contract, group area provisions etc. remains. Arrests under the Trespass Act came to 77,458 Africans in

1986.[70] Even the legal requirement for a document on the person stays, complete with fingerprinting. Indeed, the government has a whole battery of legal controls, to which reference has been made above. It may, however, be expected that these laws, which deal with the security function of the pass laws, will be phased out to be replaced by the more usual forms of control over movement used in such countries as China and the USSR, which ultimately depend on housing, jobs and the control over transport.

The abolition of formal controls providing for inequality is government policy. The government will try, as it has done, to drive a division between the urbanized and non-urbanized worker. This is likely to be successful for a limited period of time, but not forever. If industry expands and a large permanent labour force in the towns is established, its separation from the reserve army of labour would strengthen the hands of the employed proletariat. If they maintained a temporary contract system they would have changed so little that the demands would intensify. The essential controls will have to be the ones described above. They are really threefold: the maintenance of a very large reserve army of labour, secondly the division of the workforce through nationalism and tribalism and thirdly, the division of the workers between the semi-skilled and unskilled on the one side as against the more skilled and educated.

The Nature of the Capitalist Solution

There is no real permanent solution for the government or any foreseeable capitalist government. The main effect of the government policy, which is in fact that of the international bourgeoisie, is to remove many of the most obnoxious controls over the black petite bourgeoisie and the educated professionals. The construction programme in the towns will clearly benefit them as well as a layer of the semi-skilled and skilled black workers. The South African government has begun to privatize the building societies in order to provide housing for blacks in the townships. The money so raised can provide the structures while a suitable small number of blacks receive mortgages.

Afraid of a socialist revolution in South Africa, with the enormous consequences that it would have on the whole of Africa, and the rest of the world, the bourgeoisie has decided to find a bourgeois end to racial discrimination. Unfortunately, for them there is no easy solution since, as we have argued, racial discrimination has become the regulator of accumulation itself. To disentangle it today and introduce a welfare state/incorporated black bourgeoisie type solution is difficult. The London *Financial Times* put this point in the course of a leader arguing against punitive sanctions as follows: 'The dangers of failure are obvious: more strife with no guarantee that the end result will be the replacement of apartheid, or at any rate its replacement by a more acceptable system.' Earlier in the article it points out 'they may stir up an already unstable situation in South Africa without furthering their cause.' 'Great political skills', it announces, will be needed to ensure the middle way between white supremacy and the unmentionable.[71]

The only certain method is a political deal with Gorbachev together with substantial aid to South Africa, such that the five million whites would not lose too heavily while a section of the blacks would receive access to good housing and consumer durables. The importance of the USSR lies both in its influence on the surrounding territories and on the ANC. Then a base would be established for a black/white government which would maintain capitalism for a few more years. It is still not clear that such a deal can be struck, although the certain outcome of the present events is that the blacks will be defeated for the time being and the concessions won will be divisive although real.

Given the strength of Stalinism and the influence of the capitalist powers, only three outcomes to the mass eruptions of 1984–6 were possible. One was the defeat of the 1984 insurrection followed by an attempt to introduce a black/white capitalism. A second scenario is that of minimal change as after Sharpeville. Whites would remain in charge but blacks would have increasing access to skilled jobs, better housing and increasing welfare state benefits. The third possibility is that an eventual deal is struck with the ANC but that the US is too weak to enforce its own solution and Stalinism does indeed rule for a time, on the basis of a market and limited nationalization. This outcome is unlikely to last very long for the reasons indicated above, but it may be long enough to shorten the lives of the leaders of the left. The methods by which the South African Communist Party has dealt with dissidents in the past would have made the late unlamented Joseph Stalin proud.

The first possibility is that of a delaying type of solution. That is indeed what is being and will be implemented. The demands of the foreign bankers amount to the creation of an African middle class, together with the implementation of a welfare state for a section of the workers. A crash programme of improving black housing for those already in the towns by both equipping the existing housing with running water and electricity and building more flats/houses, the provision of other benefits such as health and education, the placing of the black middle class on to the boards of companies and the arrangement of real companies to be at the disposal of black entrepreneurs in the so-called white areas, are the conditions for relative stability in South Africa. Anglo-American has implemented its own plan by 'an imaginative scheme aimed at fostering black owned businesses by giving them supply contracts.'[72] Objections by whites have been firmly rebuffed.

It is entirely possible that the large reserve army of labour will attract foreign capital to areas such as the homelands. The homelands have the attraction that they are well policed, politically stable and have ample supplies of cheap labour. The problem for such capital is the relatively low level of education of the workforce. This adds urgency to the need for a vast improvement in educational provision for the majority of the population. That Taiwanese and other investors should have put money into the 'homelands' is not surprising but the low productivity of South African labour and the limited market limits such investment.

The implementation of the reforms enumerated requires a settled investment climate. For this purpose all opposition from the blacks as well as from the whites must be smashed. Then the concessions can be made. The white lower middle class, bureaucrats, artisans and the few genuine white workers would find that taxation had increased and inflation, which has run close to 20 per cent per annum in the post 1985 period, would be intolerably high, while unemployment among whites would inevitably increase. The resulting revolt by the whites, which has already become widespread, would mean that the government would have to either rule by decree, or use the army against that section of the whites.

Thus, in the period after 1986, the government has embarked on a campaign of terror. Ordinary militants and others have died unknown deaths. The situation has become desperate for the ordinary worker. By 1989, the government had succeeded to the extent that it was freeing some of those imprisoned.

Manipulation of the electoral system, which still provides a gerrymandered majority to the Nationalist Party, could provide an electoral gloss. The political solution, which must involve universal suffrage, has not been easy for the Nationalist Party to implement. Nonetheless, once the ANC has abandoned guerilla warfare, embraced the United States, and market forces, there is no obstacle to it merging with so-called liberal whites such as the former leader of the Progressive Federal Party, Van Zyl Slabbert. The technical difficulty of placing all the blacks in South Africa on the electoral roll together with the exclusive nature of the white urban areas would probably ensure that there were enough representatives elected who would both support capitalism and a gradual structural change in South Africa. Blacks then could be accepted into white areas provided they had the money.

Such a complex of concessions could be implemented but it has to be said that the chances of long-term success are no greater than the chances of an untrained tightrope walker trying to make it across the proverbial rope. That does not mean that a temporary success will not be scored, through the gradual introduction of a black capitalism. Unfortunately, the international anti-apartheid campaign is leading in that direction.

This discussion is continued in the last section on Strategies for Change.

8

The World Economy, Imperialism, Colonialism and Racial Discrimination

The key questions in South Africa have three dimensions. There is, firstly, the inter-relation between the class and the colonial bond, secondly, the connection between colonialism and racism and thirdly, the relationship between the South African socio-economic variation of the capitalist system and the evolution of the world's political economy. These three aspects are only detailed forms of the inter-relation of the movement of the law of value and the class struggle. The capitalist/worker relation given by the process of extraction of surplus value is constantly modified in its working by the nature of the class struggle. The law of value itself has its own movement and after reaching its mature form must necessarily begin a process of decline, epitomized in the evolution of modern finance capital. The declining form of value, finance capital, in turn, inter-relates and reacts with the class relation. South Africa has evolved a peculiar form of social relation precisely in the epoch of finance capital.

The crucial feature of the epoch of finance capital in this regard has been the need to contradict the essence of capitalism by deliberately accepting the division of labour such that abstract labour is broken up into two or more sections. By so doing capitalism has become noticeably less efficient, less profitable and more political. South Africa, from this viewpoint, is merely one example, an extreme example, of a feature of the epoch.

Jack Simons has drawn attention to the problems, and to the connection between racialism and capitalism. In particular, he draws attention to the importance of the British aristocracy of labour. What he failed to do, and for this he cannot be blamed, given the times and his environment, is solve the puzzle of the relation between colonialism/racialism and capitalism. This is not an historical question but one of political economy. His solution is simply to state that the whites acted as a cohesive group to protect their interests, within capitalism. There is thus a feudalistic structure imposed on capitalism. What is not explained is the reason why the whites were successful, in political economic terms and not in historical terms. Why was the capitalist class of the United Kingdom prepared to make such a concession?

They were prepared to lose profits for the sake of apparent stability, even before the epoch making 1922 strike. This is not explicable only in terms of the internal relations of South Africa. Nor is it explicable in terms of the colonial bond. On the contrary, from the point of view of the British capitalist class the development of a colonial middle class, aristocracy of labour, or internal bourgeoisie constituted nuisances they could have done without.

There is an argument which runs as follows. The British ruling class were extracting the money commodity, gold, from a part of the empire, which enabled the United Kingdom to maintain its dominant international financial role at a time when its industrial position was already greatly weakened. The lower rate of profit occasioned by the concessions in South Africa was, therefore, offset by the global advantages presented by the control over the money commodity itself. In other words, it was the nature of finance capital, which was less interested in industry and more in making money out of whatever activities, that accepted the racialism.

Yet it was not only gold that was extracted from the mines of South Africa and the Boer War was a costly enterprise politically and financially, which had to be justified. Nor can it be understood as simply a blunder on the part of the government of the Empire, or simply an attempt to impose order. Whatever the subjective motivations of the bourgeoisie, led by Rhodes, and the understanding of the Generals, there was a logic to the events. In a period when capital was being challenged in its heartlands, as Rhodes understood, and the British capitalist class was declining, an alternative source of profits and stability was required. Finance was invested in areas where returns were quick, and high, with easy repatriation to the United Kingdom. This meant for the colonies that they were to serve as a receptacle for capital only in relation to the extractive industries, agriculture/plantations or the infrastructure for that purpose. The work of Michael Barrett Brown long ago showed that this was the case for the colonies as opposed to the 'developed' countries, where investment, from the UK etc. also went into industry.

The Colonial Relationship

South Africa was a classical colony in being agricultural, having a largely extractive industry (including gold and diamonds), an unskilled workforce and large peasantry. It was, however, not so typical in having settlers from Europe, who were both the peasants and the overseers over other peasants of the economy. The problem is that these settlers were often as little educated, with as little wealth as the indigenous inhabitants and owed as little allegiance to the colonial overlord as those African peasants. The actual size of the Dutch/French/English settler population, before 1870, is greatly exaggerated in South African government histories but even the settlers after 1870, and after 1900, were not possessed of wealth, or of considerable education. Nor were they, on the other hand, simply adventurers, intent on exploiting the black majority. They were largely part of the export of labour from the continent of Europe, which was also going to the Americas.

It has also to be remembered that the white mining/industrial labour of South Africa did not initially supervise the African population, although the farmers did employ black labour. What then is colonial in the racialism of South Africa? To say that a black regime would not have accepted so many whites may or may not be true, but is irrelevant. It is not the presence of persons of different colour that is crucial, but the relationship, which uses colour/ language/culture as a means of superexploiting one section of the society. That relationship does not have to be colonial at all. The Irish have suffered from that relation in Britain, as Marx himself remarks. What then is the specifically colonial aspect?

The colonial relationship between a metropolitan country and a subordinate country or national group is founded on extraction of the surplus product from the subject grouping as a whole. It involves the extraction of surplus value, in the case of capitalism, from the national grouping as a whole. The meaning to be attached to this latter statement is that the source of the surplus value is the worker or peasant but the normal internal rate of surplus value is lowered through transfer to another country. As a result, the local capitalist class has a lower rate of profit than would otherwise be the case, or alternatively is so reduced in numbers and command over capital that it constitutes little more than local agents for an external bourgeoisie. In other words, the existence of a stunted local bourgeoisie is an indication of transfer of capital to the bourgeoisie of the metropolitan country. In this sense, of a transfer of capital to the metropolitan countries, particularly the UK, clearly South Africa is still a colony but one with a powerful internal bourgeoisie.

There is a particular problem when it comes to the wages of the workers in the colonies. They receive lower wages than their metropolitan counterparts, permitting a higher rate of surplus value even if the local agents may receive only a small proportion of that surplus value. On the other hand, the value of their labour power is nationally determined, not internationally, so that they may actually not be superexploited, though the rate of extraction of surplus value may be very high. Of course, often enough the workers were a small minority of the population, who had to be relatively better paid than the peasants to ensure their loyalty. In the non-industrial stage of extraction of surplus value the metropolitan power had no interest in preserving the lives of the workers who were then often paid below value.

However, the existence of a colony implies more than just transfer of surplus value. Historically, it has always meant a transfer of surplus value by force. It is in the end an exaction of tribute. At the present time, many third world countries transfer part of their surplus value to the United States but it is difficult to call such examples as Brazil or India simply colonies. They do have a local bourgeoisie of much greater size than before independence and they do impose restrictions on the export of capital, profits and local currency abroad. The term neo-colony does not solve the problem either, because there is a real difference between say Tanzania or Mozambique before independence and after, masked by the use of the word colony in however attenuated a form. The conclusion to be reached is that the political aspect of the international state, the Empire, is crucial. The fact that workers are still exploited in the independent countries, that surplus value is still transferred to the metropolitan countries and that these countries have only a nominal independence is all true.

They are dependent countries but their governments are locally staffed, their bureaucracies are local, they have in some cases a local capitalist class and the population usually acquires health and education facilities otherwise not provided. Their standard of living may go down, millions may be killed by their own governments and there is seldom any form of democratic control from below. Nonetheless, it is clear, however unfortunate the country, it is not the same as before independence. Socialists may recoil in horror at all these countries, but that does not make them the same as they were when they were straightforward colonies.

The view that it is impossible to achieve socialism in one country has been amply vindicated in the almost total failure of all the former colonies which call themselves socialist. They have become increasingly helpless playthings of the world division of labour and hence have become dependencies of international financial capital. It is also noteworthy that these countries have all failed to develop to the point of equality with any developed country. The IMF has had to use economic sanctions, which it is increasingly unable to enforce, since the metropolitan powers cannot now use direct force. The local bourgeoisies, elites and middle classes have felt compelled, in turn, to reject the demands of the bankers, and the finance capital establishment is now afraid of the consequences of a sustained default.

This conclusion does not mean that the extraction of surplus value from South Africa by the United Kingdom is of no importance to the history of South Africa. It signifies that such a process is different from the traditional colonial process. The provision of capital for the United Kingdom by South Africa during the Second World War was part of the Imperial system, which involved, *inter alia*, blocking accounts in the sterling area, but it was undone by the Nationalist government on coming to power. The point that has to be taken into account is that South Africa was both a colony and not a colony and that the racial discrimination which has evolved did so against the wishes and needs of the colonial masters. There should be no confusion between the racialism of the colonial representatives, reflecting a global elitism, and that of local settlers whose racialism was normally total precisely because they were the direct extractors of that surplus value, rather than an overlord receiving part of the locally produced surplus value.

The difference between a superexploited black man in the US, or a superexploited Spaniard in Switzerland and a superexploited colonial worker in pre-independence Nigeria is instructive. Although the superexploitation in the developed countries is assisted by the state it does not actually depend on direct force for its maintenance. The fetishism of the commodity plays the crucial role. The worker works because he has to feed his family and can only do so in this particular way. The skill and capital required to alter his position are not available to him. He sells his labour power for the only price that is available. That it is below value cannot be altered. It cannot be altered collectively because of the atomized nature of the work force.

The colonial worker, on the other hand, also has to sell his labour power or starve, but normally he has had the alternative of staying a peasant, or acting politically against the barriers preventing him receiving higher wages. Governments, like the British in South Africa, have forced peasants off the land through compulsory taxation and maintained control over workers in the towns with the army or police. India, too, was an occupied country until independence. Economic measures such as a poll tax have no meaning unless backed by force. Such a poll tax is very different from local income tax where there are economic sanctions.

When we turn, however, to the case of a 'settler economy', such as contemporary South Africa, the relationship is closer to that of the Black in the USA, Spaniard in Switzerland, Moroccan in France, Turk in Germany. In both cases there are superexploited and privileged workers *in situ* but in South Africa the majority are the superexploited as opposed to the metropolitan cases cited above, where the privileged workers are the majority. It has also to be noted that the majority of workers, in South Africa, are indeed superexploited, paid below the value of their labour power, and not just receiving wages less than their counterparts in Western Europe, as has been true of other countries in

Africa. Paradoxically in the latter case, the colonial case, the wages of workers in those countries could actually be less than the workers in South Africa. The reason for that paradox is that the entire workforce in South Africa has been brought into the modern industrial economy and consequently has to be paid accordingly.

The maintenance of control over the majority requires a strong state, but it only needs the strong state because of the concession to the minority of privileges over the majority. It is not the colonial control but the demand for a share of the surplus value that has forced the metropolitan and later local bourgeoisie to introduce and maintain the racial discrimination. It is here that we see the real difference between South Africa, a colony and the metropolitan instances. In the case of South Africa, the wage differences have been so great as to make all talk of whites also being workers, mental or manual, open to question. Workers who received between three and twenty times the wage of a black worker, usually when acting as supervisors, are not capitalists but then they are not simply workers either. South Africa, therefore, constitutes a particular blend of a colonial past, with a modern capitalist economy founded on racial discrimination.

The argument may be summed up as follows. Racial discrimination and apartheid are not simply features of a colony. If that were so, then the same argument applies to blacks and the discrimination against them in the US. The colonial masters prefer, by and large, to build up a local elite or bourgeoisie, which has some degree of popular support. In the twentieth century, a colony in which a racial minority ruled was clearly doomed to revolution or chaos. On the other hand, in Kenya, Rhodesia etc. the United Kingdom did use the settlers as economic and political rulers but they did not shut out the potential black middle class. Nor did they have the same problem to the same degree of white workers. The whites of Kenya and Rhodesia have done very well in the independent states of Kenya and Zimbabwe. For the majority of whites in South Africa their only future under black rule must involve a considerably worse standard of living. The fundamental question is thus of the industrialization of South Africa and the break up of abstract labour to the point where there are actually two separate abstract labour components of the workforce, with one, the whites, receiving surplus value from the other.

The colonial question is of historical significance only. That the whites came from outside of Africa is irrelevant to any internationalist or humanist. That some of the whites came with particular skills and that the blacks were not quickly given those skills is of crucial importance but not immediately traceable to racialism. The blacks were peasants while the imported skilled workers were accustomed to discipline in an industrial environment. The blacks were a conquered people who would clearly revolt, and did so, when possible. There can be little doubt that the white management had a racialist attitude but not one that overrode the question of profits, amply proven by their replacement of expensive white labour with cheaper black labour when the time came. South African history can only be understood in terms of its colonial formation, but the imperial expansion of Europe also involved the extermination of large numbers of indigenous inhabitants as in Canada, Australia, the United States and elsewhere. This racialism is different from racial discrimination against a section of the working class. The former is colonialism and was also employed in South Africa, but the latter is a modern form of control over the working class.

The role of gold was as a source of profits of an easily realizable commodity but it was not the only source of profits. Gold has also been countercyclical and helped to stabilize the class which held the gold mines. South Africa cannot, however, be explained only through the peculiarities of the money commodity.

Imperialism and South Africa

South Africa exhibits the characteristics of both a modern dependency and those of an independent metropolitan country. It transfers surplus value to the metropolitan country but on the other hand it limits that transfer in time, amount and category. It does not have the threat or presence of foreign troops. It no longer has imperial bases on its territory. It has considerable investments in other countries, most particularly the United Kingdom, the United States, Canada, Australia, Brazil and elsewhere. It maintains control or has a dominant economic position in Southern Africa. The jargon of the Soviet style theorists is one of a sub-imperialist power, whatever that may mean.

It has to be noted that the word imperialism as used by Lenin referred to the export of capital from the imperialist powers of Europe. In return, the metropolitan powers received cheap imports, providing the necessary profits. In fact history turned the original form on its head in that the empire exported its own surplus value and so capital to the metropolitan countries, allowing the United Kingdom to become an increasingly rentier, or finance capitalist country. The capital was not simply re-exported or left in the exploited country but employed by the British imperial masters in the home country to maintain an aristocracy of labour, ignore the needs of industry and import industrial goods from other countries, and live a good, gentle and aristocratic life. The rentier/finance capitalist position was maintained by re-investing wherever the profit was highest.

Thus the characteristic of a dependent territory, as discussed in the previous section, has to be that of transfer of surplus value to the bourgeoisie of another country. Such transfer may take place through interest, dividends, profit, rent, transfer pricing or some other method. It may be processed through finance capital or through industrial capital or for that matter through the state. (There are dependent territories, which have no economic function but service the political needs of the superordinate bourgeoisie, such as strategically located islands. They do not involve any change in the definition as they only serve this function in order to secure the transfer of the surplus value of other territories.) Such a dependent territory is not necessarily in the position of a colony, controlled by the state of a another country in order to secure the necessary transfer of funds, and it has a considerable degree of latitude, contingent on the relationship of the respective bourgeoisies.

South Africa is definitively a dependent territory on this definition. It is not, of course, necessary to use this word as it has been employed by the dependency school. It has also to be re-affirmed that capital is effectively not being transferred or exported to the dependent territory but on the contrary it is the latter territory that is losing capital to the metropolitan country. It has further to be observed that the control is not exercised by multinational companies or through possession of technological superiority in themselves. The fundamental relation is through a transfer of surplus value to the metropolitan country in virtue of the control of capital in that dependent country, control over the international market in the commodities sold by that country or control over the imports of that country. Methods of exercising this control are various and need not be discussed here.

Turning to South Africa, the controls exist through ownership of capital internally, through the international market in South African exports and through the supply of machinery and other imports to that country. On examination, however, it appears that since the main export of South Africa is gold, no real control exists over that commodity since it is the money commodity itself, and it is impossible to do much about restricting its import or influencing its price simply to affect South Africa. Furthermore, diamonds are in fact controlled by the diamond syndicate, which is entirely in the hands of the South African firm, De Beers. Thus it is not through control over export prices that control is exercised, though the pricing of imports still allows for transfer of value, largely to Europe and America. Its extent is greatly limited by the relatively industrialized nature of the country, permitting it to substitute its own manufacture or bargain with different firms in different countries. The fundamental nature of that dependence then lies in its provision of invisibles, largely to the United Kingdom. It is not of course really a question of the balance of payments, so much as the proportion of profits provided for UK companies. That has been reduced of late by the decline in profitability of companies in South Africa.

The feature then of South Africa is that it transfers surplus value to a limited degree to metropolitan powers and that transfer has historically involved control over imports, exports and internal profits, but that has gradually diminished. It has been declining for many years to the point where the real connection has become more complex. In other words, it is surely possible for the South African bourgeoisie to invest sufficient internally in order to cause a decline in the total value exported by a substantial sum. Anglo-American has enormous investments in the major metropolitan countries and could offset its foreign investments against metropolitan holdings in South Africa. It does not do so because it wants to diversify outside its origins, most particularly because of the risk of possible change in that country. Hence the dependency began in the colonial status of South Africa and moved away from that situation to a point where diversification took the form of investment externally or simply exporting capital by the South African owners.

It would then appear that the real reason for this dependency is the insecurity of capital. As a result, it is not able to form a true indigenous capital and has to form a strong alliance with international capital.

The Eccentric Case of the 'Internal Colony' Argument

The Communist Party of South Africa put forward, in the late 1950s, the hitherto unknown theory of internal colonialism and hence that the blacks constituted such an internal colony.[73] The whites were the colonial power controlling the blacks. It is true that, on the definition above, which was not the definition of the CP, the whites extract surplus value from the blacks. It is also true that an apparatus of force is required to maintain the blacks as suppliers of labour power.

Nonetheless, the same statement could be made of any working class in revolt against their ruling class. The feature of a colony is that extra surplus value is extracted from the working class/peasants, in effect a rent, via the local agents, whether landlords, an internal bourgeoisie or simply the superordinate state apparatus. This super surplus value is not then distributed to an aristocracy of labour, leaving the bourgeoisie of the imperial power no better off, but rather is absorbed into the general rate of profit in the metropolitan power, making it higher than it would have been in the absence of a colony. If the bourgeoisie chooses to buy off a section of its metropolitan workers this action is performed much as a master will give some leftovers to his dogs. He definitely does not give the dogs the meat itself.

The argument above has gone to show that there is no evidence that the superexploitation of the blacks actually does go to raise the general rate of profit, compared to what it may have been in the absence of racial discrimination. The very high salaries of the whites and the overall costs of apartheid offset the extra surplus value so extracted from the blacks.[74]

It has also to be added that the categorization of what can more easily be termed a case of superexploitation of one section of the working class to the benefit of another (and of a petty bourgeoisie) in one country has no similar example in colonial history. If, for example, the Ukraine is called an internal colony of the USSR, as has been argued, it is then stated that extra surplus product is being siphoned off from Ukrainian workers which then goes to the Soviet elite for distribution at their pleasure, whether on arms, their luxuries, or on Moscow factories. Whether this argument is true will depend on whether the Ukrainian workers are superexploited or not. If they are not, but the surplus product still flows out of the Ukraine, then some other word than colony may be appropriate to describe the inferior position of a section of the USSR. No one tries to argue that all Russians are better off because of the Ukrainian situation. On the contrary, many Russians are actually worse off than Ukrainians, although since Chernobyl that is open to question.

It may well be objected that the argument has been exclusively economic and that colonial subjects have been oppressed socially and culturally as well. This is true though it has to be noted that the apartheid regime would like nothing more than to ensure that blacks had knowledge only of their own languages. The economic power rests with a class with an alien language and culture from most though not all the exploited. The fact that some (the so-called coloured population) have the same culture as the Afrikaners is some indication of the weakness of the argument. Britain was conquered by the French speaking knights of William the Conqueror in 1066, and Britain is not regarded as having been divided into an internal colony and a ruling class.

Can a country consist of an internal colony and a separate ruling class with no other working class? Classes require their opposites. The South African capitalist class must have a South African working class and vice versa. It is not absurd to extend a reality of all ruling classes, that they have their own internal language and culture, to the extreme of South Africa. The language and culture of the capitalist class is always dominant, sweeping away the everyday language of the ordinary worker, whether, to take the example of the United Kingdom, he be Scottish, Irish, Welsh or Cornish, unless there is a determined resistance movement. In Switzerland, up to half of the real working class of that country comes from other countries and speaks other languages than the dominant one of the canton.

Nonetheless, only a dogmatist would try to impose the simple capitalist/worker division on South Africa. I have not tried to do so, arguing in terms of a capitalism regulated by racial discrimination. There is also a real national question.

9

The National Question and Working-Class Divisions

The rejection of the absurd internal colonialism argument does not mean that there is no problem of a national kind. The country is clearly peopled by a number of different national groupings. As already remarked, the Soviet Africanist Potekhin argued for a division of the country according to the dominant national group of the region. Does South Africa constitute one nation or several nations? Does South Africa have one culture or several and what attitude would a liberated regime take under these circumstances? Much heat has gone into these questions in South Africa. What will happen will happen and it is fruitless to speculate. Potekhin was obviously taking the example of the USSR in the abstract, for the reality of the USSR is the dominance of the Russian language and of Russia, to the point of burgeoning nationalist movements expressing extreme hostility to Russia.

It would be logical to conclude that the industrialization of the country has left it with a tendency to the formation of one culture, imposed effectively by the ruling class. The working class has no culture as a working class, and its abolition as a class upon emancipation means that its demands are not for the imposition of a culture of its own, which ultimately can only be that of a slave culture. Yet the African population does not only constitute a working class, for they are obviously also a conquered people who have been forced into wage labour. All the old tribal structures have been so corrupted that they must be considered either means of control or archaic. Capitalism has destroyed the old mode of production totally, contrary to the rather peculiar and passé views of such as Wolpe, but racial discrimination has ensured that the old languages, customs and sense of community are retained. Had South Africa gone the way of Brazil, which was not impossible at one point, the normal atomization of commodity production would have destroyed that sense of community and much else with it.

It is hard to conclude that South Africa does not constitute a single nation, if a non-Stalinist definition is adopted. It has a single political economy, part of the international division of labour but sufficiently independent within it to constitute its own entity. The territory is a single economic, social and political unit. The crucial and decisive aspect is that the socio-economic framework of South Africa is an integral component of the world economy. The fact that peasants and workers may speak different languages among themselves and are separated from the ruling class by language is neither here nor there. The idea of the Afrikaners going off to exist on their own is absurd. How can a state bureaucracy go off on its own? What, we may ask, of the different African language groupings? Clearly there are a whole series of different ethnic groupings in South Africa but they cannot exist as independent nations any more than the blacks or the Italians could in the United States.

A liberated South Africa would clearly be a black ruled country, since they are the majority, and a socialist South Africa would quickly integrate the whole population into a democratic culture, with councils, elections, different factions, views and parties. The common language(s) as opposed to local language(s) would have to be selected by popular decision making. The essential point, however, is that the common economy has already integrated the population into one entity, in spite of the so-called homelands. That the whites would either leave or have to change their jobs and accept a lower standard of living is a matter of necessity, which does not alter this argument.

Stalin's definition of a nation was much used in South Africa but it provides little enlightenment and much obscurity. Essentially that is because his definition of a nation is a simple definition and not a dynamic description of an entity. To put it mildly it is no more Marxist than is the statement that nation is spelt n-a-t-i-o-n. That a nation has to have a common economy, territory, language and culture says precisely nothing, when the real cases may have none or only one of these factors. Did the Ukraine have all these things in common? Was not the Ukraine part of the territory and economy of a greater Russia? Only the peasants of the Ukraine had a Ukrainian culture. What of the case where the ethnic group had no territory and yet manifestly had its own language and culture? Its importance lies in the programmatic acceptance of the need to grant the right of nations to self-determination, which was not in fact granted to either Georgia or the Ukraine. If every nation has a right to self-determination and there are several nations in South Africa on the Stalinist definition, then the struggle in that country is not only Balkanized but doomed. Stalin's definition is not just useless, for it is multi-factoral, as opposed to essentialist and as such basically liberal.

Another viewpoint is that of Neville Alexander, who is both a major political activist and theorist in South Africa. He has developed a theory of what he terms colour-caste relations, adapted from theorists in the United States. He argues that whereas the struggles in South

Africa are class struggles that is not the nature of consciousness in South Africa. The participants in the class struggle perceive reality in colour-caste terms. Alexander is anxious to get away from the use of the term race which in itself he sees as being either useless or reactionary. In his critique of various liberals he points out that their analysis has at best only a descriptive validity and no explanatory power. In this he is correct but it is not at all clear why a term like colour-caste succeeds in providing any explanation at all. Marxists, and he is undoubtedly a Marxist, must proceed not from definitions but from political economy. The term caste derives from a social formation which Marx characterized as a form of the Asiatic Mode of Production. Unless caste can be reconciled in some way with value both objectively and subjectively, it cannot do more than describe forms of discrimination. It cannot add to an understanding of the contradictions in the society and so the source of movement in South Africa.

Alexander's weakness lies in his critical acceptance of Althusserianism, through the work of Therborn and other modern Althusserians.[75] As a result he is forced to look at reality in structural rather than dynamic terms. He even uses concepts derived from Maoism, one of the sources of Althusserianism, like antagonistic and non-antagonistic contradictions. The very use of such terms displays a total ignorance of dialectics. This was understandable in a Stalinist leader like Mao, who, as Holubnychy has shown, could not read Marx, since his works had not been translated into Chinese, but not in someone like Alexander who is a modern Trotskyist with access to the literature.[76] The problem with the use of colour-caste is that it does not assist in understanding the dynamic of South Africa. The fact that workers in South Africa perceive themselves as black workers or coloured workers or as whatever colour does not alter the fundamental dynamic of the country, but it does require to be explained on the basis of that fundamental dynamic. Women workers may perceive themselves as female workers, exploited by men, and Mexican workers as Chicano workers exploited by Americans, Palestinian workers as Arabs exploited by Israelis, this does not mean that they constitute new social or political categories.

On the other hand, as we argue above, it is odd that Alexander only derives the consciousness of the black workers from South Africa itself and not from a more general nationalism, which has had more to do with Stalinism than anything else.

The question is not the term which could just as well be race, nation or caste but the origins and source of movement of the divisions opened up. It is quite clear that the origins of racial discrimination do not arise out of the Asiatic Mode of Production. It is equally clear that the relatively static nature of that mode of production essential for the reproduction of caste is absent in South Africa. The utility of the term, according to Alexander, lies in its explanation of the integrative nature of the divisions in South Africa. In other words, racial discrimination serves to divide the class and maintain the capitalist system by uniting workers with non-workers. Apart from the obvious point that one does not need another term to make this argument, if Alexander had not been blinded by Althusserianism, which after all is only a modern Stalinism, he might have sought an explanation for consciousness in the nature of value itself.

There are numerous works on the nature of ideology but there is little that has integrated ideology with value itself. Yet that is Marx's method and approach. The ideology of capitalism is not Protestantism or any form of religion but commodity fetishism.

Althusserianism and its modern followers like Therborn, Callinicos and others have either rejected the labour theory of value or severely qualified it. They have also rejected Hegelian type contradictions and characterized theories based on such views as reductionist. As a result, they and their followers, who are quite influential in South Africa, provide an explanation for consciousness from within itself. It is indeed easy to reject a simple economistic view that racial discrimination arises out of the need to extract super profits. It is not, however, either Marxism or even simple human reasoning to argue that there is a one to one relation between ownership or the extraction of profits and the forms of the extraction of the surplus product. It is just Stalinism, now so extensively debunked as a viewpoint and as a theory inside its unfortunate home, the USSR. Alexander would have done well to ignore these modern defenders of Stalinism and proceed from first principles.

If we look at the commodity in South Africa and so commodity fetishism, we observe that the dominance of the commodity over the human being and so over the worker is the dominance of a white commodity. It is a machine standing over the worker, which he must associate with the white foremen; it is the sale of his labour power to the enterprise, which is necessarily white owned; it is the purchase of commodities from shops which are not usually black owned. White workers, in competing with black workers to sell their labour power, have invented forms of protectionism, which are only an acceptance of the rule of the commodity labour power over their lives. Dehumanized both by the sale of their labour power and by the forms of control over their labour power in the labour process, workers are divided in reality and so ideologically. All the modern alternatives to class struggle can be traced back to the commodity and its fetishization. As argued above, in the section on the political economy of racial discrimination, these new forms derive from the need to patch up the holes in commodity fetishism, arising from a declining capitalism. As a result, they are both of commodity fetishism and they are not.

Nationalism, sexism, racialism are all means of dividing workers, which owe their success to the reality of worker atomization and so competition, to the powerlessness of the seller of labour power, who then uses surrogate forms of collectivity, acceptable to the capitalist class. The socialization of labour necessarily demands the coming into being of a collectivity, but that collectivity can only exist at the point of revolution. Before that point the dominance of the commodity ensures that many distorted and harmful forms of integration can come into being.

Many scholars and students have been confused by the work of Lukács. He produced a curious mixture in arguing on the above theme.[77] On the one hand, he stood on Marx's view of the revolutionary collectivity of the class, while on the other he put forward a Weberian view of commodity fetishism. The Lukácsian theory of reification deviates from Marx both in being non-specific to capitalism and in being idealist. He sees reification as the imposition of a set of rules on the human being. As a theory then, reification is not linked to value and its movement. As a result, Marxists have tended to consign fetishism to reification and so to a sociology as opposed to a political economy. Nonetheless, the understanding of racial discrimination and the racialist ideology which accompanies it is to be sought in the differential sale of labour power and control over the labour process.

Some writers have argued that the division of the class argument is too simplistic. They fail, therefore, to see that a united class would be a united collectivity of the vast majority against the capitalist class. Such a unity could only be suppressed by force and then only for a limited period of time. As a result, the capitalist class has only one weapon, the division of the class, or put differently: prevention of the class coming into being as a collectivity and so as a revolutionary entity. What is complex is not the division but the method of division. It is, therefore, necessary to refine the argument.

When the worker can see through his domination by the commodity and possesses the power to overthrow that domination, alternatives have to be found. The alternatives, however, can only derive from the same source, even if in a distorted form. A successful nationalism, for instance, leads to unity within the nation with the consequent domination of the workers by their own national capitalists. Even before the formation of the new state, the nationalist workers accept the division of exploitation between that of one group of capitalists and another. Such a capitulation to exploitation as such can be explained as the result of failure to see beyond commodity domination, or as the result of such control over the product and labour process that the worker grasps at straws.

The argument above does not detract from the necessary discussion of the attitudes of black and white workers. The real problem is that, while those views are relatively easy to find and document, their underlying meaning is not at all so easy to discover. Much of the history which has been written up to now tends to avoid a more profound explanation of the particular class relationships in South Africa. Many historians and analysts have preferred to document attitudes and struggles rather than penetrate below the surface reality.

Alexander, however, has done the movement a service in pointing to the integrationist nature of the system in South Africa. The term colour-caste implies a single national entity, as in India, divided by caste like divisions based on colour.

10
Strategies for Change

The Communist Party line has been nationalist from the early 1950s onwards, as opposed to standing for socialism to be achieved through independent working-class action. John Saul has illustrated the degree to which it has now attempted to adjust itself to present day reality by declaring that it stands for the two stages, first abolition of discrimination and then socialism, in the form of a merged relation of stages. If racial discrimination arises out of capitalism there can be only one stage in any revolution. It is not a question of permanent revolution (Trotsky) or of continuity in revolution (Lenin) as there are no feudal remnants to overthrow. If, on the other hand, the Stalinist conception of popular front is adopted then, as with the two stages of the overthrow of Fascism, state-monopoly capitalism, and every other real case, there is a first stage followed by a second stage. Rejection of a popular front leads directly to demands for socialist revolution based on the black workers, if racial discrimination is capitalist and only capitalist.

If it is not just capitalist but something else, then there is the possibility either of the permanent revolution variant or of a two stage revolution. The two stage form consists of a nationalist first stage and then a second socialist insurrection or other form. It differs from the permanent revolution in that the latter does not just say that the socialist revolution follows but that the socialist revolution is necessary to maintain the first stage at all. In that sense the two stages are one continuous whole. The Communist Party line has been consistent for the past thirty years in refusing to bow to its own members who wished to start from the necessity of a working-class revolution. The increasing power of the working class and the intense demand for socialism has forced the Communist Party to produce what is little more than a smokescreen for its continuing nationalist and *de facto* anti-working-class line.

To see the difference that would occur we just have to consider the ANC/Communist Party line in contrast with a socialist one at the present time. In the period 1984 to 1989, it stood for organization in the townships, for armed warfare on that basis and for a series of nationalist demands encapsulated in the so-called Freedom Charter. On the other hand there were members of that same CP as well as the anti-Stalinist left who argued that guerilla warfare was a diversion from the real possibility of change. The emphasis had to be placed on the working class as a class and on building it up underground with or without trade unions. A powerful working class would hold the capitalist class to ransom over the one question that concerns it, that is the level of its profits. In the course of that struggle the white worker might rebel but he could only lose, and when he did so the whole state would become entirely unstable.

Following the nationalist/Stalinist line the struggle is based on the black townships in alliance with the black bourgeoisie and petty bourgeoisie. It has clearly failed since the only point of warfare was in the areas where the oppressed themselves live. The rate of profit has hardly been touched. The withdrawal of foreign loans is quite another matter. The alternative is to concentrate on the point of production and subordinate the community strife to that of the class struggle. It would also have the advantage that the organs of struggle could be subject to democratic control at the point of production, through election of workers' committees and councils. At the present time the forms of struggle are popular but not democratic while the ANC/CP is arguably wholly undemocratic.

The Relationship between Moscow and South Africa

It may be churlish to criticize a party which has already been forced to change by instruction from the USSR. Moscow has apparently announced that it wants political change without the use of armed force.[78] It has snubbed the ANC, when it visited the USSR, and conducted direct talks with South Africa.[79] When the South African Foreign Minister, Pik Botha, could admit to the legitimate interest of the USSR in South Africa, announce that he had had discussions with the USSR, while contrasting the attitude of Gorbachev with that of the ANC/CP, it has to be said that the process of South African stabilization is proceeding apace.[80]

The relationship between South Africa and the USSR is not difficult to understand. The USSR has always accepted, in a mirror image of Botha's view, the legitimate interest of the United States in South Africa. It is not about to embark on a war with the United States over one of the most mineral rich countries in the world. A perusal of Soviet journals over the past 20 years, under the different Soviet leaders, shows a consistent line. The USSR has called for the elimination of apartheid and so-called national liberation. In practice this can only mean black capitalism. It might also mean a black capitalism which was not anti-Soviet if the USSR was successful, but that is all it means. The USSR has thereby obtained a bargaining chip of no mean size. In return for providing the necessary guarantees to the United States that South Africa would not go socialist, the United States can reduce its pressure on the USSR and find methods of providing finance for the dependent superpower. In this instance, the USSR is actually selling out its ally the ANC, and local CP, as it has done to so many other parties and socialist groups in the world, since Stalinism ruled the USSR. However, anyone who could read Russian would know that it always had intended to do so.

The particular strategy of armed warfare was one which the former leadership used in imitation of the first fully Stalinist Comintern line of class against class. This pseudo-revolutionary line was intended to pressurize the United States, when the latter was attempting to squeeze the USSR to come as a supplicant to the bargaining table.

On the one side, the Brezhnev regime was trying to maintain internal stability by changing as little as possible, conceding to workers, ignoring the intelligentsia's material interests and suppressing the writings of the same intelligentsia, while on the other it was protecting itself by maximum external expansion. The two policies are complementary, in that the external expansion diverts the interest of the United States and provides a certain internal and external support for the regime.

The formulators of the foreign policy of the United States in fact colluded with the Brezhnev regime in maintaining its stability. Contrary to certain current defenders of the former NATO policy, the effect of the harsh NATO policy of increasing pressure on the USSR, was to increase the national support for the regime. The NATO powers appeared as aggressors intent on increasing military expenditure beyond all reason. In turn, the Brezhnev regime could expand the military sector and so ignore the interests of the population, while obtaining their tacit approval. This also meant support for liberation movements around the world in their armed struggle against the governments of their countries. Once, however, the bubble burst and the Soviet regime attempted to find a solution to its dire economic problems, all external adventures appeared as unnecessary and too costly to sustain.

That the USSR never intended to go very far in South Africa is neither here nor there. It can deliver a very important guarantee to the United States, as the guarantor of world capital, and that is to the effect that the major mass movement in South Africa will prevent the working class taking power. It cannot, in fact, deliver over very many years but then the bourgeoisie will accept remission as being as good as a cure.

Those who stand for socialism must, therefore, accept that the USSR stands on the other side, together with the United States and liberals of the South African government. Any fight for socialism is necessarily a fight against those forces and so against those who support the

ANC/CP strategy. It is true that the USSR has disappointed its allies in the ANC/CP and there will be many of its members who will move over to the left given time, but before the ANC splinters, crumbles and becomes a governing party they will only constitute a barrier to real change.

The Penumbra of South African Stalinism and the Alternatives

John Saul's argument, in his *New Left Review* article, and not only his argument, amounts to the acceptance of a theory and form of struggle which is wrong, undemocratic and anti-socialist. He says: 'What can be affirmed here is that the establishment of a positive dialectic between "popular democratic" and "proletarian" moments is perfectly possible – and perhaps even essential to successful revolution in South Africa.'[81] In his article he has found a reason why elements of the left, like himself, who are critical of the USSR, of Stalinism, of the lack of democracy in the ANC/UDF/CP should support the CP line since it involves some element of working-class participation and the potential of democracy. He appears to ignore totally the reality of power in South Africa and the world. Unless there is somehow a break with the SACP and unless the ANC becomes democratic, which it is certainly not today, the ANC in power would mean a Stalinist state. If alternatively and more likely the ANC splits with the bourgeois–democratic wing taking power then there would be a period of capitalism without the political trappings of apartheid. There is absolutely no basis for John Saul's optimism even in terms of the overthrow of the system, since the very tactics employed, of nationalist struggle, have failed, at a not inconsiderable cost to the population.

The reality of the present is shown in the forces shaping the 1989 South African government budget. On the one hand, it has increased expenditure on the police by 30 per cent, on the army by 22 per cent and on the other it is increasing expenditure on education by 19 per cent. Even with a 15 per cent and more inflation rate, these figures show a policy of repression combined with the development of a black middle class. The raised sales taxes, with relatively stagnant real wages, imply that sections of the white workers will have to provide the sacrifices necessary to build up the black middle class. It is a delicate operation to attack the manpower of the South African state, while attempting to establish a new social base for the system in South Africa.[82]

Since the bourgeoisie accepts the need to change in order to avoid socialism, the socialist movement has to demand immediate and total abolition of all controls over labour and the labour movement. It has to establish solidarity between labour movements and not between capital, bankers, and the opposition. The demand of workers in South Africa has to be, as it increasingly has come to be the case, for a truly socialist South Africa as part of a socialist world. In view of the rapid decline of Stalinism in its homeland, the USSR, it is not impossible that the South African working class will dispense with the tutelage of a weak CP though that time is some years hence.

Can a non-racially discriminatory capitalism come into existence in South Africa? In principle, capitalism could dispense with racial discrimination but in its decline it is not easy to dispense with a method of control over the working class. It is even more difficult to remove a form which is critical to accumulation itself. The conditions required for such a change are two in number. Firstly, there has to be an alternative form of division of the working class, and secondly the effects of racial discrimination would have to be disentangled from the nature of accumulation in South Africa. The first point requires that there be a black bourgeoisie, a highly paid black white collar group, a welfare state for all and no doubt national/tribal divisions. The second would need the stranglehold of the Oppenheimer empire to be loosened, a machine tool industry to be established, large scale manufacture of durable consumer goods to be entrenched, and for all goods to be on a par technologically and in term of quality with the best in the world. South Korea has gone part of this road so one would expect that South Africa, which has extraordinary advantages in terms of raw materials etc., would also be able to follow. In fact, it is unlikely precisely because South Africa is more advanced than South Korea in the development of its proletariat. It is most unlikely that an alternative division of the proletariat be found and hence the centralization of capital would have to be retained. As a result, neither the competition of capitals nor the incentive system employed in developed capitalism could operate to the degree required. South Africa would remain a stunted capitalism, which would remove formal discrimination only to retain a reality of black workers and white employers. Whites would not be protected by law but they would have both the education and capital necessary to rule. The large absolute number of blacks who would come to staff bureaucracies and the professions would be a very small proportion of all blacks, and hence could not control the majority of the population for very long.

Indeed, it is more than likely that such a formally black capitalism would be more ruthless with the black working class since they would not have either international sanctions or a nationalist threat to worry about. Furthermore, they would be less secure and more determined to succeed in the new free market culture. The fact that ultimate control of capital would remain with whites would not alter this situation. It is already evident in Zimbabwe, Kenya and elsewhere in

Africa. Clearly this would not be apartheid and there would be no legal racial discrimination but the real situation would not have altered for the better for the vast majority of South Africans.

Would this not still be racial discrimination?

Tables

South African Statistics

Table 1: Growth Rate of Real Gross Domestic Product

Table 1(a)

Average annual change, percentage:	
1911–19	–2.0
1920–29	6.9
1930–39	5.0
1940–49	3.4
1950–59	4.3
1960–69	5.8
1970–79	3.1} see below
1980–87	1.3} see below

Source: Jill Natrass: *The South African Economy: Its Growth and Change*, OUP, 1981, p. 25 and SAIRR, *Survey of Race Relations*, 1987/88, p. 406.

Table 1(b)

Real GDP growth, percentage:	
1970–74	4.7
1975–85	1.8
1980–85	1.1
1977–88	2.1
1980	5.6
1981	4.8
1982	–0.8
1983	–2.1
1984	5.1
1985	–1.2
1986	1.0
1987	2.6
1988	3.2

Table 1(c)

Annual per Capita GDP Change, percentage:	
1950–1959	2.0%
1960–1969	3.0%
1970–1979	0.5%
1970–1984	−1.4%
1980–1987	−1.1%
1970–1987	0.0%

Source: *Financial Times*, April 2nd 1986, supplement on South Africa, p. V, *Financial Times*, 12 June 1989, supplement on South Africa, p. VIII, SAIRR, *Survey of Race Relations*, 1987/8, p. 406, 290.

Table 2: Manufacturing Industry

Table 2(a)

Total Earnings as per cent of value added:	1970	1983	1984	1985
South Africa	46	52	50	50
United Kingdom	52	44	44	45
United States	47	39	40	40
Germany	46	48	48	46
Brazil	22	20	20	20

Source: The World Bank: *World Development Report 1988*, Oxford University Press, Oxford, p. 239.

Table 2(b)

Fixed Capital Stock
Real percentage growth. 1975 prices

Period	%
1957–64	7.0
1964–69	8.0
1969–74	8.3
1974–80	5.9
1980–84	4.0

Source: T.C.Moll: 'Probably the best laager in the World', The Record and Prospects of the South African Economy, in *Can South Africa Survive?* John D. Brewer (ed), Macmillan, London, 1989.

Table 3: Investment in South Africa

Table 3(a)

South Africa's Foreign Liabilities
Rands million:

1985	1986
81,420	71,904

Source: SAIRR: *Race Relations Survey*, 1987/8, p. 111.

Table 3(b)

US Investment in S.A.
Direct Investment:*

1966:	$490 million
1981:	$2.6 billion
1983:	$2.3 billion

Post tax return:
1980:	30%
1984:	7%

*At the end of 1984, S.A. investment accounted for slightly more than one per cent of U.S. foreign investment.

Source: *SA Financial Mail*, August 23, 1985, p. 56.

Table 4: Population of South Africa (millions)

	1987	1951
African:	26.1	8.56
Coloured:	3.1	1.10
Asian:	.91	.37
White:	4.9	2.64
Total:	35.2	12.67

Source: SAIRR, *Race Relations Survey*, 1987/8, p. 11, *South Africa 1984: Official Yearbook of the Republic of South Africa*, Chris van Rensburg, 1984, Johannesburg, p. 26.

Table 5: Employment

Table 5(a) By sector

1987, in thousands
Totals including whites (brackets exclude whites)

Sector:	Total	Total excluding whites
Manufacturing:	1,325	1,000
Mining:	759	(680)
Public Sector:	1,669	1,000
Construction:	294	259
Electricity:	57	34
Finance:	160	43
Trade and Catering:	740	479
Agriculture:	1,200	

Table 5(a)(i) Manufacturing Industry

Employment:

1970:
Total: 1.171 million workers of all races.

1987:
Total: 1.325 million workers of all races.

African:	705,000	53%
Asian:	88,500	7%
Coloured:	237,400	18%
White:	294,500	22%

Increase 1970–87 = 11.6%

Source: D. Hobart Houghton: *The South African Economy*, OUP, 1976, p. 289, SAIRR: *Survey of Race Relations*, 1987/8, p. 322.

Notes:
1. Average number employed per establishment in 1976 was 88. Source: Jill Natrass, p. 169.
2. In the period from 1919 to 1976 'the output from the machinery-making subsector had grown at an average annual rate of 14 per cent, to provide 13 per cent of the sector's total output'. Jill Natrass, p. 169.

Table 5(b) Economically active African population by industrial sector, excluding the so-called homelands of Transkei, Bophuthatswana, and Venda, in 1980, per cent

Agriculture:	18.6	(1970: 35.8%)
Mining & Quarrying:	12.8	
Manufacturing:	13.8	(1970: 9.9%)
Electricity, gas, water:	0.8	
Construction:	4.7	
Commerce:	9.7	
Transport & Communication:	3.2	
Finance:	1.0	
Services:	22.6	
Unemployed & other:	12.8	

Source: South African Institute of Race Relations: *Survey of Race Relations in South Africa* 1982, Johannesburg, 1983, p. 70.

Table 5(c) Economically active population: excluding Transkei, Bophuthatswana, Venda and Ciskei (TBCV)

	1981	1987
White:	1.945 million	2.009
Coloured:	.865	1.184
Asian:	.260	.345
African:	6.580	6.921
Africans in TBCV (1981)	1.3	

Source: SAIRR 1982, p. 69–70, and SAIRR, *Survey of Race Relations*, 1987/8, p. 292.

Table 6: Nominal Levels of Payment to Employees

Rands per month.
Note: The rand has fluctuated from around 2 rands to the British pound in 1981–2 down to almost 5 to the pound in 1990. At purchasing power levels the rand would probably be closer to 2.5 to 3 to the pound and 1.2 to 1.6 to the US dollar.

Table 6(a) Claimed average household income, 1982

African	204
Coloured	548
Asian	819
White	1380

Ratio of African to White households: 14.8%

Source: SAIRR: *Survey of Race Relations in South Africa*, 1983, Johannesburg, 1984.

Table 6(b) Median pay at different levels of skill, 1983, % of white pay in brackets

	Unskilled	Semi-skilled	Skilled
African	351(56)	524(65)	849(60)
Coloured	383(65)	618(77)	990(70)
Asian	428(73)	681(85)	1187(84)
White	589(100)	797(100)	1407(100)

Unskilled African/ Skilled white = 24.94%

Source: SAIRR: *Survey of Race Relations in South Africa*, 1983, Johannesburg, 1984.

Table 6(c) Average monthly earnings: 1986

1986:	Rands	as % of White Earnings
African:	500	28.8
Asian:	912	52.7
Coloured:	634	36.60
White:	1732	100

Source: SAIRR: *Survey of Race Relations*, 1987/8, p. 289

Table 7: Balance of Payments

Balance of Payments: 1987–8
Balance of Trade:

	1988	1987
Exports:	$22,432 million	$21,088
Imports:	$17,210 million	$13,925

Gold exports: (1988)
  $8,527 million or 38% of total exports including gold.
Current account balance: 1988: $1,272 million
                           1987: $3,002 million
Debt owed to other countries: $21,680 million (1988)

Source: *Financial Times*, 12 June 1989, Supplement on South Africa, p. 8.

Notes and References

1. S.P. Bunting: At the 6th Comintern Congress, 1928, with an introduction by Baruch Hirson, *Searchlight South Africa*, no. 3. pp. 51–83.
2. My information, admittedly oral, is that the real correspondent with Trotsky was Jacob Burlak, who was the major theoretician of the group.
3. The white worker/black worker division is crucial but there are, of course, black/black divisions. The latter play their own role and as is argued below, it was, in principle, possible for the capitalist class to have utilized such black/black divisions, as the prime division, had no other form of segmentation of the workforce been present. There is no discussion in this book of the other colour groups, not because they play no role but because their role is subordinate to that of the determining division of the working class.
4. Abstract labour is discussed in some detail in a section below.
5. For instance, COSATU made this statement in its constitution: 'employers in South Africa continue to make massive and completely unrealistic profits when compared with employers in other capitalist countries.' *Review of African Political Economy*, no. 36, 1986, p. 82. 'Apartheid ... is a system of economic, social and political relations designed to produce cheap and controlled black labour, and so generate high rates of profit.' Robert Davies, Dan O'Meara and Sipho Dlamini: *The Struggle for South Africa, A Reference Guide to Movements, Organisations and Institutions*, vol 1, p. 2.
6. The principal Althusserian protagonists are Harold Wolpe, who fundamentally supports the CP viewpoint, and articles of the kind discussed in the footnote 14 below, which refers to an article by Davies, Kaplan, Morris and O'Meara. It is amazing that Althusserianism should have become so important in South Africa at all. For an outline of some of the different currents of thought in South Africa see A. Callinicos: 'Marxism and Revolution in South Africa', *International Socialism*, no. 31, Spring 1986, London. A more general account of the literature is provided by Michael Burawoy: 'State and Social Revolution in South Africa, Kapitalistate', *Working Papers on the Capitalist State*, no. 9, Berkeley, pp. 93–121, and 'The Capitalist State in South Africa: Marxist and Sociological Perspectives on Race and Class', *Political Power and Social Theory*, no. 2, 1981, pp. 279–335. Burawoy sees the state as an arena of struggle rather than the organ of repression of the ruling class. He also looks at sections of the capitalist class as using, maintaining and discarding racial discrimination.

7.   Leo Kuper has made mincemeat of most of the so-called Marxist approaches in his work *Race, Class and Power*, Duckworth, London, 1974, pp. 205–10.

8.   Merle Lipton: *Capitalism and Apartheid*, Gower, London 1985.

9.   The London *Times*, 31. 03. 86.

10   Lipton, *Capitalism and Apartheid*, p. 101.

11.   H.J. and R. Simons: *Class and Colour in South Africa, 1850–1950*, Penguin, 1969, p. 618: 'South Africa uniquely demonstrates that a dominant racial minority can perpetuate social rigidities and feudalistic traits on an advanced and expanding industrial base.' The odd thing about this statement is the non-class approach adopted by the former leader of the left wing of the Communist Party, and hence of the Communist Party before 1950. Jack Simons commanded wide respect in Southern Africa, and indeed educated a whole range of the left in the subcontinent. The problem arises because the kind of Marxism exemplified by Stalin in his *National and Colonial Question* has no history or political economy.

12.   No Sizwe: *One Azania, One Nation, The National Question in South Africa*, Zed Press, London, 1979. No Sizwe is in fact Neville Alexander.

13.   See for instance: I. Potekhin: *Formirovanie Natsionalnoi obshchnosti yushnoafrikanskkikh Bantu*, Akademii Nauk, Moscow, 1955, p. 6, P.M. Shastitko, *Sto let bespraviya*, Moscow, Vostochnaya Literatura, 1963, p. 142, and *Katzenellenboigen: Yuzhnoafrikanskoye zoloto i obostreniye angloamerikanskikh protivorechii*, Politizdat, Moscow 1954, p. 12.

14.   Harold Wolpe: *Race, Class and the Apartheid State*, James Currey, London, 1988, pp. 28–35. This is the latest statement of Wolpe's position in support of the Communist Party's internal colonialism thesis, liberally supported with quotes from Joe Slovo and the latest declarations of the Communist Party itself.

15.   Frederick A. Johnstone: *Class, Race and Gold, A Study of Class Relations and Racial Discrimination in South Africa*, Routledge and Kegan Paul, London, 1976, p. 202.

16.   Rob Davies, Dan O'Meara, Sipho Dlamini: *The Struggle for South Africa, A Reference Guide to Movements, Organizations and Institutions*, Zed Books, London, p. 2.

17.   O.C. Cox: *Caste, Class and Race*, Monthly Review Press, New York, 1959.

18.   See a detailed outline of the history of growth rates by D. Kaplan: 'Beyond the Indicators: A Perspective on the South African Economy', in *South African Review* no. 4, Ravan Press, Johannesburg, 1987.

19.   For manufacturing see Table 2(b), for mining: S. Herbert Frankel: *Investment and the Return to Capital in the South African Gold Mining Industry*, 1887–1965, p. 8, where he finds 'the average rate of return from 1935 to 1963, in money terms, was 4.3 per cent for gold mining as compared with 7 per cent for United Kingdom Equities.' It is noteworthy that it is in the pre-1935 period that the return is higher. While Frankel's averaging techniques and categories are flawed, it is quite clear that capital certainly did not regard investment in the

gold mines as anything other than as one of many comparable places to invest, with similar rates of return. This, indeed, is Frankel's fundamental conclusion.

20. W.M. Freund: 'Race in the Social Structure of South Africa, 1652–1836', *Race and Class*, vol 18, no. 1, p. 62.

21. Robyn Rafael, 'Job Reservation on the Mines', in *South African Review* no. 4, Ravan Press, Johannesburg, 1987, p. 266.

22. The article, cited in the footnote above, gives the impression of a continuous history of discrimination almost from the origins of the Gold Mines in the Transvaal. The question is not whether blacks were worse off or in worse positions but whether there were extra-economic forms of exclusion of blacks from particular jobs. Rafael points to examples in the Boilers and Machinery Law of the South African Republic, and the Mining and Regulations Law of 1896. He also does point out that the latter law did not exclude blacks from blasting competency certificates, although blacks were not in fact granted certificates. Later, of course, in modern times this became a primary legal blockage to black advancement. The point, however, is that these are the usual laws cited to provide the continuous history, which thereby appears a natural history. What is not cited is the relative absence of legal restrictions compared to the period after 1924.

23. For what must be one of the best surveys of labour in the mines before 1914, see 'Labour in the South African Gold Mining Industry, 1886–1914', Peter Richardson and Jean Jacques Van-Helten, in S. Marks and P. Rathbone (eds), *Industrialisation and Social Change in South Africa*, London, 1982. The authors show in considerable detail the complex relation between mine owners and the different sections of the labour force. In particular, they point to the importance of mining costs for the employers' strategy. They also make the point that the employers were concerned with the threat that African workers would learn to strike, and worse, from the white workers' strikes of 1902, 1906, 1907 and 1913. (p. 93)

24. The crucial role of the international decline of capital and the nature of its weakened state is not generally stressed. Duncan Innes and Martin Plaut, however, in their reply to the Althusserian/Poulantzian school, 'Class Struggle and the State', *Review of African Political Economy*, no. 11, London, 1978, p. 56 have this to say of the immediate post-war period: 'This intensification of militancy among black workers ... developed under conditions in which capital in South Africa found itself weakened internationally by the ravages of the war and confronted by the revolutionary crisis that developed at the time of the Bolshevik Revolution in Russia.'

25. Innes and Plaut, ibid.

26. The discussion took place over a number of journals but included the *Review of African Political Economy*, no. 7, Davies, Kaplan, Morris and O'Meara: 'Class Struggle and the Periodisation of the State', an article which exemplified the use of Poulantzian/Gramscian/Althusserian

concepts, with the same disastrous results that those concepts have had in other fields. Wolpe is of the same persuasion, but in a different current of the overall tendency. He argues strongly against them. On the other hand, the authors posed important questions which have still not properly been answered. They received exhaustive replies from Simon Clarke: 'Capital, fractions of capital and the state: "neo-Marxist" analyses of the South African state', *Capital and Class* no. 5, and the Innes and Plaut article noted above, with Belinda Bozzoli in the same issue of the *Review of African Political Economy*.

The industrialization of South Africa is not due to the arrival of national capital or fractions of manufacturing capital, which themselves have to be explained. Nor does national capital necessarily industrialize a country, still less manufacturing capital. India has industry and national capital but is certainly not industrialized. South African industrial growth has more in common with the kind of growth which was made mandatory in the world after the Second World War. Keynesianism, reformism or concessions to the working class were essential after the Second World War. In South Africa, it was apparent that full employment for whites was a necessary precondition for stability. This required industrial growth. The local capitalist class then worked with the state to industrialize the country. It is dubious whether national capital existed in South Africa in the 1920s. The category itself can only be applied with difficulty to South Africa, since crucial capitalists, like Oppenheimer, have a British or international orientation, within South Africa. South Africa, in this respect, is closer to Canada and Australia.

This book rejects the view that the differing sections of capital in mining, industry, or agriculture are to be seen as warring *per se*. As argued in the text, these sections are only separated precisely because of racial discrimination, which leads to differing rates of extraction of surplus value from these sectors. This in turn is based on the differing natures of abstract labour in these sectors. If there were no racial discrimination and mechanization proceeded to its natural conclusion, these different sectors would have no real differences. In other words, the apparently more radical stance of manufacturing capital is more one of impatience than a real difference in interest.

27.   Baruch Hirson, in a recent issue of the journal, *Searchlight South Africa* no. 2, 'A Question of Class, The Writings of Kenneth A. Jordaan', has drawn attention to Kenneth Jordaan's contributions in the history of South African Political Economy, which include the view, according to Hirson, that South African industrialization was necessarily racialist. While certainly an important statement, it is too general to have clear consequences. If it is stated that racial discrimination was the only means by which South Africa could be industrialized, then it is open to question. If it is stating that the capitalist class is necessarily racialist in South Africa then it is obviously untrue. On the other hand, if it is stating that South Africa industrialized in a racially discriminatory way and that accumulation was necessarily of this

kind, then, as I have been arguing, it is clearly correct. Can a non-discriminatory capitalism exist in South Africa then? It would seem that Jordaan would answer in the negative.

28. *South African Journal of Economics*, June 1985, p. 143.

29. *Financial Times* 16.03.1989, p. 4.

30. See Belinda Bozzoli, *The Political Role of a Ruling Class, Capital and Ideology in South Africa, 1890–1933*, Routledge and Kegan Paul, London, 1981, Chapter 4. She describes the process whereby 'imperial capital' was weakened relative to 'national capital' in the post First World War situation. Whether one agrees with her categories of hegemony and factions of the ruling class is another matter.

31. For a discussion of the role and control of Oppenheimer see (1): Duncan Innes: *Anglo-American and the Rise of Modern South Africa*, Heineman, 1984, p. 229ff.

To see the meaninglessness of divisions in the SA ruling class, we can look at the holdings of the Anglo-American group. It is estimated that Anglo has some 56 per cent of shares on the Johannesburg Stock Exchange and the next biggest company, Barlow Rand, some 7 per cent. The latter, however, is 20 per cent owned by AAC. There are officially five independent mining houses, but only Anglo-Vaal, the smallest does not belong or have substantial shareholdings held by AAC, either directly in the relevant mines or in the mine holding companies.

Anglo-American is dominant in industry, banking and even commerce, through its industrial, financial and commercial subsidiaries. By 1976 'Anglo group companies held top positions in every one of South Africa's economic sectors except agriculture'. Innes, p. 221. It was Anglo-American that assisted Afrikaner capital in 1963 to obtain a strategic interest in mining, when they helped Federale Mynbou acquire General Mining. It was a political stroke which ensured that Afrikaner capital would ally itself with the interests of capital in general. It led to a political shift in the Nationalist party itself. Dan O'Meara: *Volkskapitalisme, Class, Capital and Ideology in the Development of Afrikaner Nationalism, 1934–1948*, Cambridge University Press, 1983, p. 250.

(2): Edward Jessup: *Ernest Oppenheimer: A Study in Power*, Rex Collings, London, 1979.

As an illustration of his devotion to business we may note the following comment of the biographer: 'He had lived through anti-German, anti-Jewish pogroms twice already and it made good business sense to become a Christian: he controlled 90 per cent of the world's diamonds and if diamonds were vital for the Allied war machine, Germany's need was no less vital and as the world knows Hitler would not knowingly trade with a Jew.' (p. 316)

The book is a useful description of how a family managed to obtain control over the South African economy through ruthless attention to the necessities of profit.

(3) David Pallister, Sarah Stewart and Ian Lepper: *South Africa Inc. The Oppenheimer Empire: The secrets behind one of the most influential organisations in the world*, Corgi, London, 1988. 'The picture is essentially one of a relatively small economy with three main pillars: the state, the three insurance-based groups slugging it out with each other, and Anglo. Small wonder then that Anglo is the final arbiter in the private sector and that the Oppenheimers inspire awe in their own community.' (p. 38)

32. For a different explanation and a detailed study of the causes of the centralization and concentration of South African capital see Innes, *Anglo-American*, pp. 219–222 and p. 237. He seems to argue in classical Leninist terms of the growth of monopoly capital.

33. All figures cited here come from the 1983 *Survey of Race Relations* of the SA Institute of Race Relations, Johannesburg 1984, pp. 108 ff.

34. Raymond Lotta: 'The political economy of apartheid and the strategic stakes of imperialism', *Race and Class*, vol 27, no. 2, 1985, pp. 17ff.

35. Figures cited here come from the 1983 *Survey of Race Relations* of the SA Institute of Race Relations, Johannesburg 1984, pp. 108 ff.

36. See for instance: Ann and Neva Seidman: *U.S. Multinationals in Southern Africa*, Tanzania Publishing House, Dar es Salaam, 1977. The book indicated the expansion of American capital without providing any kind of substantial justification for the thesis that American capital is supplanting British capital.

37. Charles Harvey: 'British Investment in Southern Africa', *Journal of Southern African Studies*, no. 1, London, 1974, p. 52.

38. Statistics from:
a. *Financial Times*, April 2, 1986, South Africa, pp. II and IV,
b. *International Financial Statistics*, August 1985, p. 422,
c. *Financial Times*, March 3, 1989.

39. *Financial Times*, March 3, 1989, p. 4. Report by Anthony Robinson.

40. *Financial Times*, 20.1.1988.

41. The South African Foundation was established to promote South Africa abroad and build closer relations between sections of capital and the Afrikaner middle class. 'The advent of the South African Foundation reflects the return of big business to active politics.' ... 'to pave the way to the merger of the two white sections' ... I, Harry Oppenheimer, by A Special Correspondent, p. 14, *Africa South*, vol 4, no. 3, Cape Town, 1960. The writer argues that Oppenheimer effectively saw to it that opposition was of a moderate kind. It is, of course, believed that the leader of the anti-Government organization of ex-servicemen, the Torch Commando, Sailor Malan, was assisted to retire to a farm. The point, however, is that there is absolutely no evidence that the capitalist class took firm measures to oppose the South African state. If anything there is evidence to show support for it.

42. *The Economist*, 1st July 1989, 'The Oppenheimer Empire, South Africa's family affair', p. 75. Main Street refers to the headquarters of Anglo-American.

43. Harold Wolpe, *Race, Class and the Apartheid State*, Chapter 1.

44. *Race Relations Survey* 1985, South African Institute of Race Relations, Johannesburg, 1986, p. 143. They quote the results of the Human Sciences Research Council survey published in March 1985.

45. For a more modern discussion see Archie Mafeje: 'Soweto and its Aftermath', *Review of African Political Economy*, no. 11, p. 23ff., London, 1978.

46. S.P. Bunting: At the 6th Comintern Congress, 1928, Baruch Hirson: 'Bunting vs. Bukharin: The "Native Republic" Slogan', *Searchlight South Africa*, no. 3, July 1989.

47. B. Hirson: *Yours for the Union, Class and Community Struggles in South Africa*, Zed Press, London, p. 80.

48. ibid.

49. I. Potekhin: *Formirovanie Natsionalnoi obshchnosti yushnoafrikanskkikh Bantu*, Akademii Nauk, Moscow, 1955.

50. H.J. and R.E. Simons: *Class and Colour in South Africa, 1850–1950*, Penguin, 1969, p. 581.

51. ibid., p. 598.

52. B.M. Hirson: *Yours for the Union*, Zed Press, London, pp. 187–188.

53. ibid.

54. Simons and Simons, p. 263.

55. The Communist Party, its close relations with the USSR and its infiltration policy are described by Kurt M. Campbell: *Soviet Policy towards South Africa*, St. Martin's Press, New York, 1986. Its climb to power in the ANC is described on page 39. For discussions on the interaction of the Communist Party and the ANC, as well as Soviet policy, see also Peter Vanneman: *Soviet Strategy in Southern Africa, Gorbachev's Pragmatic Approach*, Hoover, Stanford University, California, 1990. While these books are written from a highly contentious viewpoint they do operate using genuine source material. Unfortunately the ANC and the Communist Party have themselves been less than forthcoming in describing their real relationship.

56. 'Dream come True', Martin Jacques interviews Joe Slovo, *Marxism Today*, March 1990, p. 19.

57. *The Observer*, London, 27.03.89, describes Moscow policy. It includes the immortal reply of Gennadi Gerasimov, the Moscow spokesman, who when asked about the Soviet attitude to ANC violence, guerilla warfare, replied by asking: 'What violence?' He was in a way correct, since the activities of the ANC in South Africa have included only sporadic bombing, which has had very little effect. The point, however, is made that the ANC/CP will be told to desist from such violent activities as it does indulge in and come to a political deal.

58. *Pravda*, Moscow, 15.7.1969.

59. *The African Communist*, London, First Quarter 1989, pp. 109–110.

60. *The African Communist*, London, Second Quarter, 1989.

61. *The Times*, London, 13.03.1989.

62. *Race Relations Survey*, Institute of Race Relations, 1987/1988, Johannesburg, 1988, p. 460.

63.   For an early outline of the function of the Pass Laws see H.J. Simons:
      'Passes and Police', *Africa South* vol.1, no. 1, Cape Town, 1956.
64.   For an account of the laws which are usable against Africans who wish
      to enter the towns see *Race Relations Survey*, 1987/8 op. cit. p. 469.
65.   See the Table in the appendix above on the rates of unemployment.
66.   *Race Relations Survey*, 1987–1988, p. 292. Some estimates of
      unemployment over a decade are as follows:
      A. July 1, 1985: Port Elizabeth – Uitenhage – 56 per cent blacks
          Estimated 60–70 per cent of those unemployed were so because of
          recession. Source: *SA Financial Mail*, August 23, 1985, p. 74.
      B. 'There can be no doubt that the unemployment is a major reason
          for the unrest'. Professor M. Levin, Vista University, Port Elizabeth,
          SA Financial Mail, August 23, 1985, p. 74.
      C. Official estimate in 1978, May–August was 10 per cent for blacks
          and coloureds. Natrass, p. 56. Official figures put 497, 000 blacks,
          70,000 whites, as unemployed in August 1985. *SA Financial Mail*,
          22 November 1986, p. 101.
      D. Some academics estimate the total unemployed at 2.5–3.0 million.
          Survey of Race Relations in South Africa, 1983, p. 132.
      The actual numbers considered unemployed depend on the
definition employed. There are two main considerations here. Firstly,
whether workers are regarded as seeking employment. For instance, it
is common for government statistics, the world over, to exclude
women in the home on the grounds that they are not actually seeking
employment. It may be noted here that COSATU claimed in April
1988 that 'for every unemployed male worker in South Africa, three
women were without work'. The effect of this exclusion may be seen
by the huge discrepancy between government statistics and those of
independent researchers. The official version was of 17 per cent
unemployment among blacks in 1987 as opposed to an estimate of 37
per cent of all those unemployed provided by Dr. Bethlehem, the
economics consultant of the Johannesburg Consolidated Investment
Company. Other figures are even higher.
      In the second place, those engaged in subsistence agriculture and in
the homelands may or may not be regarded as unemployed. Thus one
estimate put the number of unemployed Africans as 5.5–6 million.
Another estimate put half the so-called homelands population as
being unemployed. The official estimate of around seven million
economically active Africans in South Africa has to be added to the
homelands population, who would be actively seeking work if given
the chance. There are officially six million persons in the latter area.
Assuming that around at least 1.5 million would work in 1988, that
puts the economically active population at nine million and with
figures of four to six million unemployed, the level of unemployment
is from below 40 per cent to near 70 per cent. No exact figure is
possible since the total population is not accurately known, and the
proportion of Africans in the homelands who work in the rest of
South Africa is not given for the current years. The level of

unemployment, based on reasonable human aims of providing employment for all persons from 18–65, is obviously very high in South Africa. Quite apart from the recent recession, levels of unemployment have been rising as the numbers required for agriculture both in the 'white' and old 'reserve' areas have declined. Population growth has of course also been rising fast.

67. *Race Relations Survey*, 1987–1988, p. 295. In 1980, it was estimated that 2.17 million black South African employees were considered foreign workers in the non-homeland areas (that is residents of the nominally independent bantustans). Of these 295 thousand were workers from other surrounding countries. A further 1.374 million black workers were considered South African labour in the homeland areas. In this way only three million out of 6.5 million black workers could be regarded as South African. Source: *South Africa 1984: Official Yearbook of the Republic of South Africa*, Chris van Rensburg, Johannesburg, 1984, p. 247.

While such a form of control is in no way compatible with the deal being struck with the ANC, the divisions can still be exploited.

68. The mechanization of the mines is taking place relatively painlessly, from the point of view of the mine owners, in that the higher cost mines are being closed and replaced with new gold mines, 'which will be highly mechanised and provide fewer jobs than the older, conventional operations.' *Financial Times*, Supplement on South Africa, 12th June 1989, p. VI.

69. *Financial Times* 16.03.89

70. *Race Relations Survey*, 1987–8, p. 461.

71. *Financial Times*, 4th April 1986.

72. *The Economist*, July 1st 1989, 'The Oppenheimer Empire, South Africa's family affair', p. 75.

73. The major theorist of this curious viewpoint has been Harold Wolpe. A debate ensued twenty years after the invention of the concept, around his work. The major criticism was of his Althusserian view of different modes of production. Harold Wolpe: 'Capitalism and Cheap Labour Power in South Africa', *Economy and Society*, vol 1, no. 4, Routledge and Kegan Paul, London, 1972. For an up to date version of his views see the earlier reference to his book, *Race, Class and the Apartheid State*.

74. See Table 2(b), where it is shown that in manufacturing the proportion of value added going to earnings is actually higher in South Africa than in the United Kingdom or in the United States, among other countries. Nor are tax rates lower in South Africa.

75. For a history and a critique of Alexander see Alex Callinicos: 'Marxism and Revolution in South Africa', *International Socialism*, London, Spring 1986, pp. 51–2. Callinicos accuses Alexander of 'Ideologism'. He does not discuss his theory of colour–caste.

76. This confusion is further seen by his ambiguous attitude to the USSR, where he speaks of having: a 'global policy' which 'consists, theoretically, of propagating and facilitating the world socialist revolution.' That Gorbachev does not have such a policy is a matter

of open record but it is very difficult to argue it for any Soviet leader from Stalin onwards. He makes a dubious distinction between theory and practice. If the doctrine of socialism in one country meant anything, it certainly meant that the USSR was not interested in world revolution, except to prevent and contain it. Neville Alexander: *Sow the Wind, Contemporary Speeches*, Skotaville, Johannesburg, 1985, p. 107.

77. G. Lukács: *History and Class Consciousness*, Merlin Press, London.
78. *The Independent*, 17th March 1989, p. 8.
79. The London *Times*, 13.3.89
80. Pik Botha was interviewed on *BBC Newsnight*, 15.3.1989.
81. John Saul: 'The Question of Strategy', *New Left Review* no. 160, p. 13, London, 1986.
82. *Financial Times*, 16.3.1989.

Bibliography

Alexander, Neville: *Sow the Wind, Contemporary Speeches*, Skotaville, Johannesburg, 1985.

Bozzoli, Belinda: *The Political Nature of a Ruling Class, Capital and Ideology in South Africa 1890–1933*, Routledge and Kegan Paul, 1981.

Burawoy, Michael: 'State and Social Revolution in South Africa, Kapitalistate', *Working Papers on the Capitalist State*, no. 9, Berkeley, pp. 93–121.

_____. 'The Capitalist State in South Africa: Marxist and Sociological Perspectives on Race and Class', *Political Power and Social Theory*, no. 2, 1981, pp. 279–335.

Callinicos, Alex: 'Marxism and Revolution in South Africa', *International Socialism*, no. 31, Spring 1986.

——. *South Africa between Reform and Revolution*, Bookmarks, London, 1988.

Campbell, Kurt M.: *Soviet Policy towards South Africa*, St. Martin's Press, New York, 1986.

Clarke, Simon: 'Capital, Fractions of Capital and the State: "Neo-Marxist" Analyses of the South African State', *Capital and Class*, no. 5, Summer 1978.

Cox, O.C.: *Caste, Class and Race*, Monthly Review Press, New York, 1959.

Davies, Kaplan, Morris and O'Meara: 'Class Struggle and the Periodisation of the State', *Review of African Political Economy*, no. 7, September–December 1976.

Davies, Robert: *Capital, State, and White Labour in South Africa, 1900–1960*, Harvester, Brighton, 1979.

Davies, Robert, Dan O'Meara, Sipho Dlamini: *The Struggle for South Africa, A Reference Guide to Movements, Organizations and Institutions*, Zed Books, London, 1984.

Du Toit, D.: *Capital and Labour in South Africa, Class Struggles in the 1970s*, Kegan Paul International, London, 1981.

Frankel, S. Herbert: *Investment and the Return to Equity Capital in the South African Gold Mining Industry, 1887–1965, An International Comparison*, Basil Blackwell, Oxford, 1967.

Freund, W.M.: 'Race in the Social Structure of South Africa, 1652–1836', *Race and Class*, vol. 18, no. 1.

Greenberg, Stanley B.: *Race and State in Capitalist Development*, Yale, New Haven and London, 1980.

——. *Legitimising the Illegitimate, State, Markets, and Resistance in South Africa*, University of California, San Francisco and Los Angeles, 1987.

Harvey, Charles: 'British Investment in Southern Africa', *Journal of Southern African Studies*, no. 1, London, 1974.

Hirson, Baruch: *Year of Fire, Year of Ash*, Zed Press, London, 1979.

——.'A Question of Class, The Writings of Kenneth A. Jordaan', *Searchlight South Africa*, no. 2, London, 1989.

——. *Yours for the Union, Class and Community Struggles in South Africa, 1930–1947*, Zed Books, London, 1989.

Houghton, D. Hobart: *The South African Economy*, OUP, London, 1976.

Houghton, D. Hobart and Jenifer Dagut: *Source Material on the South African Economy: 1860–1970*, vols 1–3, OUP, London, 1973.

Innes, Duncan and Plaut, Martin: 'Class Struggle and the State', *Review of African Political Economy*, no. 11, London, 1978.

Innes, Duncan: *Anglo-American and the Rise of Modern South Africa*, Heineman, London, 1984.

Jessup, Edward: *Ernest Oppenheimer: A Study in Power*, Rex Collings, London, 1979

Johnstone, Frederick A: *Class, Race and Gold, A Study of Class Relations and Racial Discrimination in South Africa*, Routledge and Kegan Paul, London, 1976,

Kaplan, David: 'Beyond the Indicators: A Perspective on the South African Economy', *South African Review*, no. 4, Ravan Press, Johannesburg, 1987.

Katzenellenboigen: *Yuzhnoafrikanskoye zoloto i obostreniye angloamerikanskikh protivorechii*, Politizdat, Moscow, 1954.

Katzen, Leo: *Gold and the South African Economy*, Balkema, Cape Town & Amsterdam, 1964.

Kuper, Leo: *Race, Class and Power*, Duckworth, London, 1974.

Lipton, Merle: *Capitalism and Apartheid*, Gower, London, 1985.

Lotta, Raymond: 'The Political Economy of Apartheid and the Strategic Stakes of Imperialism', *Race and Class*, vol 27, no. 2, 1985 pp. 17ff.

Lukács, George: *History and Class Consciousness*, Merlin Press, London.

Mafeje, Archie: 'Soweto and its Aftermath', *Review of African Political Economy*, no. 11, London, 1978.

Mermelstein, David (ed.): *The Anti-Apartheid Reader, South Africa and the Struggle against White Racist Rule*, Grove Press, New York, 1987.

Moll, T.C.: 'Probably the best Laager in the World: the Record and Prospects of the South African Economy' in Brewer, John D. (ed), *Can South Africa Survive?*, Macmillan, London, 1989.

Murray, Martin (ed): *South African Capitalism and Black Political Oppression*, Schenkman, Cambridge, Massachusetts, 1982.

Natrass, Jill: *The South African Economy: Its Growth and Change*, OUP, 1981.

O'Meara, Dan: *Volkskapitalisme, Class, Capital and Ideology in the Development of Afrikaner Nationalism, 1934–1948*, Cambridge University Press, 1983.

Pallister, David, Sarah Stewart and Ian Lepper: *South Africa Inc. The Oppenheimer Empire: The secrets behind one of the most influential organisations in the world*, Corgi, London, 1988.

Potekhin, I.I: *Formirovanie Natsionalnoi obshchnosti yushnoafrikanskkikh Bantu*, Akademii Nauk, Moscow, 1955.

Rafael, Robyn: 'Job Reservation on the Mines', *South African Review*, no. 4, Ravan Press, Johannesburg, 1987.

Richardson, Peter and Van-Helten, Jean Jacques: 'Labour in the South African Gold Mining Industry, 1886–1914' in Marks, S. and Rathbone, P. (eds), *Industrialisation and Social Change in South Africa*, London, 1982.

Saul, John and Stephen Gelb: *The Crisis in South Africa, Class Defense, Class Revolution*, Monthly Review, New York, 1981.

Saul, John: 'The Question of Strategy', *New Left Review*, no. 160 London, 1986.

Seidman, Ann and Neva: *U.S. Multinationals in Southern Africa*, Tanzania Publishing House, Dar es Salaam, 1977.

Shastitko, P.M.: *Sto let bespraviya*, Moscow, Vostochnaya Literatura, 1963.

Simons, H.J. and R.: *Class and Colour in South Africa, 1850–1950*, Penguin, 1969.

Simons, H.J.: 'Passes and Police', *Africa South*, vol.1, no. 1, Cape Town, 1956.

Sizwe, No: *One Azania, One Nation, The National Question in South Africa*, Zed Press, London, 1979.

South African Institute of Race Relations (SAIRR), *Race Relations Surveys*, Johannesburg. Annual. Last one used in this book: 1987/88.

Stadler, Alf: *The Political Economy of Modern South Africa*, Croom Helm, London, 1987.

Wolpe, Harold, 'Capitalism and Cheap Labour Power in South Africa', *Economy and Society*, vol. 1, no. 4, Routledge and Kegan Paul, London, 1972.

——. *Race, Class and the Apartheid State*, James Currey, London, 1988.

Index